THE SITE BOOK

A FIELD GUIDE TO
COMMERCIAL REAL ESTATE EVALUATION

NOW AVAILABLE WITH SOFTWARE

The Site Book is also available with easy-to-use software developed by Tangram Corporation, a nationally recognized company that specializes in building custom models for site evaluation and market analysis. Based on the model presented in the book, the site evaluation software takes information collected from site questionnaires, assigns relative weights based on your assessment of your company and market, and calculates a final site score.

A unit price of $35.00 includes software, a set of site evaluation questionnaires, and user's manual. Tangram's site evaluation software runs on Microsoft Windows™ 3.1.

ORDERING INFORMATION

_____ Please send a copy of the **Site Evaluation Software**, including software, questionnaires, and user's manual ($35.00).

_____ Please send a copy of **The Site Evaluation Kit**, which includes a copy of *The Site Book*, software for site evaluation, questionnaires, and user's manual ($45.00).

_____ Please send additional copies of *The Site Book* ($17.99).

_____ Check enclosed made payable to Mesa House Publishing.

_____ Please bill me later.

* Add $3.00 shipping and handling for under five orders. Call toll-free number for shipping quotes on larger orders.

* Texas residents add 8.25% sales tax.

Send to: **Mesa House Publishing**
3228 College Ave.
Fort Worth, TX 76110-4045

Toll-free: 1-888-306-0060

Name: _____

Title: _____

Company: _____

Address: _____

City, State, Zip: _____

Phone: _____

E Mail Address: _____

Or, call 1-800-755-3276

THE SITE BOOK

A Field Guide to
Commercial Real Estate Evaluation

by Richard M. Fenker, Ph.D.

Mesa House Publishing
Fort Worth, Texas

Cover and text design by Jim Dodson.

Library of Congress Catalog Card Number: 95-81587

Editorial correspondence and requests for permission should be mailed to: Mesa House Publishing, 1701 River Run Road, Suite 702, Fort Worth, Texas, 76107.

This publication is intended to provide accurate information in regard to the subject matter covered. It is sold with the understanding that the publisher is not engaged in rendering legal, accounting, or other professional services.

ISBN: 0-940352-10-9

Printed in the United States of America

CONTENTS

PART 1   SITE EVALUATION: PROBLEMS AND PERSPECTIVES

Chapter 1   **Introduction** 2
The Language And Logic of Site Evaluation
How This Book Can Benefit You
Ten Easy Ways to Build a Bad Location

Chapter 2   **Defining Site Evaluation** 8
Site Evaluation and Sales Forecasting
The Relativity of Site Evaluation
Convenience and Destination Concepts

Chapter 3   **Principles and Perspectives** 14
Four Perspectives on Site Evaluation
Basic Principles

Chapter 4   **Knowing Your Customers** 22
Customer Sources
Linkages
Day Parts
Frequent and Infrequent Users

Chapter 5 Demand 31

PART 2   CUSTOMER SOURCES

Chapter 6   **Residential Sources** 36
The Convenience Zone
The Residential Zone
The Destination Zone
Demographic Reports
Using a Demographic Report

Chapter 7   **Daytime Population** 52
Employees
Shoppers

Entertainment Seekers
Other Retail Linkages

Chapter 8 **Transients** 58
Commuters
Travelers
Tourists

PART 3   IMAGE

Chapter 9 **Drop-In Features** 64
Visibility
Prototype
Access
Traffic
Strategic Position

Chapter 10 **The Physical Environment** 74
Type of Neighborhood
Quality of Surroundings
Retail Balance
Gridlock
Edge Locations

PART 4   MARKET CONDITIONS

Chapter 11: **The Market** 80
Growth Strategy
Regional Awareness
Market Penetration
Market Fit
Prototype

Chapter 12: Competition 87

Understanding the Dynamics of Competition

Direct Competition

Indirect Competition

Distinguishing Between Direct Versus Indirect Competition

Cannibalism

Business Clusters

Evaluating Competition: Finding the Balance

When There is No Competition

PART 5   THE SITE EVALUATION

Chapter 13: The Site Evaluation: A Step-By-Step Guide 102

Step A: The Question of Subjectivity

Step B: Before the Evaluation

Step C: Drive the Trade Area

Step D: Study the Demographics

Chapter 14: Using the Site Evaluation Model: A Step-By-Step Guide . . .113

Step E: Entering Data in the Model Worksheet

Step F: Applying Appropriate Weights

Step G: Evaluating Your Site: Trade Offs and Negotiations

Chapter 15: Practical Advice From the Field .142

Key Points for Convenience Businesses in General

Key Points for Destination Businesses in-General

The First Location in the Market for a Destination Concept

Adding the Second Store in a Market

Backfilling in a Saturated Market

Entering a Market With No Competition

Entering a Market With Heavy Competition

Chapter 16: A Final Word 149

ABOUT THE AUTHOR

Richard Fenker has spent nearly 20 years studying the factors that drive the success or failure of restaurant and retail locations. In a review of existing real estate models in the 1970s, Dr. Fenker became alarmed at how quickly the simple regression model, which many companies still depend on, deteriorated as a tool for evaluating new sites. Dr. Fenker addressed this problem by initiating the development of a logical approach to predictive site modeling and founded the Tangram Corporation in 1981 for the purpose of developing a scientific basis for commercial real estate evaluation.

Dr. Fenker received his Ph.D. in mathematical psychology from Purdue University in 1968. He is a professor of psychology at Texas Christian University, has authored more than 50 research publications in statistics, artificial intelligence, and other related areas, and has written six books. Dr. Fenker has also built predictive models for government agencies, such as NASA, the CIA, and the United Nations.

Dr. Fenker currently lives in Granbury, Texas, on the Brazos River.

Part 1

SITE EVALUATION
Problems and
Perspectives

CHAPTER 1

INTRODUCTION

I'm standing on a piece of dirt in Oklahoma City. It's hot. Red hot. Too hot for buyers and sellers and even for fire ants. For the past hour, I've been listening to an argument between the agent, the developer, and my client, a convenience store franchisee. They are stuck. That's why I'm here. The arguments are easy to summarize. You've probably heard them all before.

Agent: This is the only convenience store location on a major street within a mile in either direction. It's got good visibility, access, and all of the other key features that you need. It's a no brainer. You need to be here.

Developer: This is the highest growth area of Oklahoma City. In five years this will be the next elite suburb. That's why I am building this center. In three years this area will be bursting with affluent families.

Store Owner: This property is already expensive. With the low traffic volumes and sparse population, I may not get a return on my investment for several years. I've got to at least break even in the first year, or this is not a good deal.

The conversations I am hearing illustrate both the key issues involved in site evaluation and the dilemma. The different points of view make it clear that perspective, or context, has a great deal to do with the decision. Often a site is labeled good or bad, not because of the immediate site features, but because of the perspective of the evaluator. The agent may be driven by the pressure associated with closing the deal in a small window of opportunity. The developer may be focused on the long-term need to get certain key tenants in the center. The store owner may be most concerned about the bottom line during the first few years of operation. All of these differing perspectives exist within a real estate system that operates within a particular market. Site evaluation is really as much about this system and its biases as it is about the quality of various site features, demographics, or competition.

One of the favorite expressions of a regular golfing partner is, "every shot makes somebody happy." The same saying obviously applies to real estate decisions. Every deal does make someone happy. This is also the dilemma. The system works best when the deal makes all parties happy, but given the widely different perspectives and expectations of each individual involved, this may not be possible. Even when it is very much in the mutual interest of all parties for the deal to be a "win," without some objectivity in the language and process of site evaluation, a win-win situation is unlikely.

My goal for this book is to do just that: To describe the factors that determine whether and how successful a site will be for a commercial concept and to introduce a logical and objective process for evaluating those factors and determining a final site quality rating. This is a "how to" book designed to be read easily and quickly and then used in the commercial environment to make better decisions. Parts II-IV of this book (Chapters 6-12) are devoted to the language of site evaluation, namely an in-depth discussion of the individual factors that influence site quality. While these chapters do not specifically focus on the step-by-step process of site evaluation, they do introduce important information about site features, demographic features, and important interactions that will become crucial as you work through the actual site evaluation. The last section of the book (Chapters 13-16) introduces a process, or *model*, for evaluating specific sites and determining and interpreting a final site quality rating. (A computer version of this model is also available on a piece of specially designed software developed by Tangram Corporation. See software kit order form at the front of this book.)

THE LANGUAGE AND LOGIC
OF SITE EVALUATION

Perhaps you've heard the phrase "art, not science" used to describe the site evaluation process. While the complexity of site evaluation may create the appearance of art—or maybe even magic—beyond that, there's not much truth to the expression. It is true that there are strong biases involved in the site evaluation process. It is also true that the factors that determine site quality are complex and interconnected; yet, 20 years of work confirms that they are also strong, measurable, and, for the most part, logical. This logic is what allows us to build a model that presumes to predict the seemingly random outcome of interactions between customer behavior, competition, demographics, site features, and location.

To understand the process behind the site evaluation model, you must first understand the idea of a model itself. A **model**, by our definition, is just a simplified description of some part of reality that is conveniently placed in a computer or on a worksheet so that it is accessible for use. A model can be as simple as a straightforward summation, or as complex as the programs required to land a probe on the moon or forecast the weather. The key factor is that the process for determining the predicted results is systematic, consistent, and logical. Ideally, the rules that govern the model's operation are similar to the rules that actually operate in the world. For example, if good visibility and access help retail sales in a normal commercial setting in a typical city, then a good model would probably have equations or rules that force expected sales to increase as visibility or access improves.

The model for real estate evaluation presented in this book (see pages 115-117) describes a simple system of collecting data on various factors that influence site quality (a rating scale of 1-5) and then defines a mathematical process for weighting each outcome to create an overall site quality rating. While the model allows for revision in the input of information (for example, you might decide to experiment with changing the assigned relative weights or a number of other factors), the *system*, or process, for handling these numbers remains unchanged.

Like many things, while the outcome of the model (usually a site quality estimate) is very useful, it is the clear understanding of the site evaluation process itself that will be of most benefit to you in the long run.

I've been in the business of building predictive models for commercial real estate evaluation for the past 20 years. In fact, I founded Tangram Corporation in 1981 with the main objective of developing a scientific basis for site evaluation. Since then, using the models developed in house, Tangram has evaluated more than 30,000 commercial sites, not including the thousands of sites evaluated by our clients using Tangram's models. And the one thing that we learn over and over again is that we never stop learning. Every model that we build depends on the one that came before it, and every new site evaluation benefits from the thousands done before.

HOW THIS BOOK CAN BENEFIT YOU

Your own process for evaluating a site, while subjective, may already be very sophisticated and valid, or very naive. For example, you may know intuitively that in order to be successful, a convenience store needs good visibility, easy access, and a street with adequate traffic—plus a hundred other facts you know from your experience. On the other hand, you may be a small business owner opening your first shop. Your site evaluation process may not be intuitively sound or based on knowledge of the important facts. However, in both situations, beginner or expert, this book offers help in several important ways.

1. It gives you a language for describing what matters to a site evaluation and why. This language provides a common framework for communicating with agents, clients, developers, and colleagues.

2. It gives you a logical way to evaluate the relative importance of site features and to combine these ratings to provide an overall site quality score.

3. It offers a neutral position intended to serve all of the different perspectives involved in the evaluation process by accurately describing the site relative to other locations.

The goal of this book is not to take away any of your intuitive effectiveness as a site evaluator, nor does it replace the complex intelligence that is driving that intuition. Your intuitions, at whatever level, are an essential part of the best evaluation process. This book's purpose is to complement this process with a language and a method for explaining the factors that determine site quality and to give you a simple, but powerful tool to use in the field for evaluations.

, This book is written for business owners, entrepreneurs, developers, agents, brokers, real estate executives, and any other individual responsible for making objective, accurate judgments about the potential of commercial real estate. The spirit of this book is summarized by one simple phrase—NO MORE DOGS!

Ten Easy Ways to Build a Bad Location

1. Insisting on a "trophy" location near your home, despite negative demographics or poor site features.

2. Selecting a weak strategic position in a highly competitive market.

3. Forgetting the importance of crucial drive–by features such as visibility or access.

4. Selecting an out–of–the–way corner in a strip center or a side street with little traffic in an otherwise busy trade area and compounding this error by counting the traffic on the busy primary road as if it belonged to you.

5. Locating near the far edge of a retail center, next to vacant land or low–income development.

6. Selecting a location that can be easily outpositioned by a major competitor.

7. Being one of the last concepts to enter a market that is already saturated with competition.

8. Being delighted, but not bothering to find out why there are no competitors near the site you are considering.

9. Locating near a mall or other retail center that closes earlier than your normal business hours.

10. Ignoring the demographic report that suggests the residents in the neighborhoods around the site are not your customers.

CHAPTER 2

DEFINING SITE EVALUATION

Before moving along any further, it may be useful to define exactly what site evaluation means and, more importantly, what it does *not* mean. As used in this book, **site evaluation** refers to the objective assessment of the quality or suitability of a piece of real estate for a specific retail or restaurant concept. To be even more specific, site evaluation is the measurement of the relative quality of a parcel of real estate, compared to other pieces of real estate, using all of the objective and subjective information available. As the definition implies, site evaluation is a process, not a result. This book focuses on the thinking and steps required to make that process as effective as possible for you and your company.

Because the term "site evaluation" is commonly used in so many different ways, it may be helpful to clarify what I do _not_ mean by site evaluation. Site evaluation in this book does _not_ refer to the following:

1. An assessment of environmental impact or other related issues.

2. An evaluation of the architectural or landscaping components of a site.

3. An evaluation of the site from a perspective concerned with city or county ordinances such as zoning or water use.

4. A financial analysis of the site comparing costs and payment schedules with expected rates of return.

5. A sales prediction (even though the sales will depend, in part, on site quality).

SITE EVALUATION AND SALES FORECASTING

Site evaluation is often confused with **sales forecasting** or **sales prediction** (the process of predicting the expected sales volume for a particular location). While site quality is an important component of a sales forecast, the two concepts are actually quite different. **Site quality** refers to the quality of the real estate, taking into account demographics, site features (such as visibility and access), and competition. Sales volumes depend on site quality, plus many other factors such as marketing, market presence, operations, customer perception, and timing. Usually site evaluation is part of a sales forecasting system, but used correctly it represents only a part—not the entire system.

Many individuals and companies confuse these two concepts and attempt to build sales prediction models using only information about site quality (usually site features and demographics). This approach creates problems because it is very difficult to separate the part of sales that can be explained by site quality from the parts that depend on other factors. The result is a prediction model that suffers from a condition known as "shrinkage" (which means that predictions for new sites that were not included in the sample used to build the model will be less accurate than expected). The best way to prevent shrinkage is to build an evaluation system based on a true understanding of the factors that determine site quality and to avoid models based on a simple statistical "goodness of fit" measure. This book is primarily concerned with the evaluation of real estate quality, but as you will see, this takes you a long way toward accurate sales prediction.

THREE COMPONENTS OF SITE EVALUATION

A good site evaluation has three major components: clear objectives, good sources of information, and a systematic process.

The objectives of site evaluation include

- Finding the best available real estate in the market
- Comparing two potential locations
- Explaining the source of problems for an existing store
- Avoiding a mistake or reducing risk in a new location
- Supporting a scientific real estate evaluation process

The sources of information used in site evaluation include

- Demographics
- Specific site features such as visibility or access
- Strategic plans or goals
- Customer information
- Marketing or advertising support

The site evaluation process may involve

- Surveying your customers to identify who they are and how they behave
- Ordering a demographic report to see where these customers reside
- Driving the neighborhood to study business or retail activity
- Counting traffic or rating competition near the site
- Evaluating the site's potential visibility and access
- Looking for barriers or other special features
- Creating an overall site evaluation report

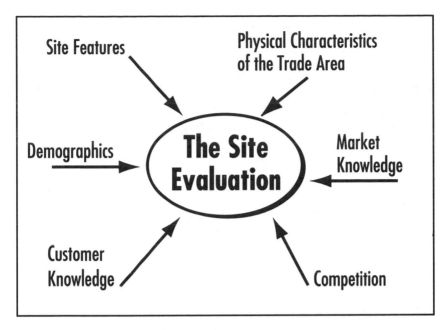

Figure 2-1

Factors that influence the site evaluation.

Some of the different factors influencing a site evaluation are shown in Figure 2-1.

THE RELATIVITY OF SITE EVALUATION

Site evaluation requires a mixture of relative and absolute judgments. Good or poor visibility is often defined relative to other retail businesses in the area. Population or a count of the number of competitors, on the other hand, is an absolute measure even though the relative value of these measures might change. For example, an annual household income of $45,000 in Granbury, Texas, puts your family well above the mean, while in Washington, D.C., or Orange County, California, you might be below average. The most important relative judgment in a site evaluation is that of *site quality* because this measure gives you a direct comparison between a potential location and other locations throughout the market.

Site quality is a composite score computed by combining the scores for individual site features and demographics into an overall quality scale. In other words, after collecting a variety of information on a site, you must somehow combine or "add it up" to get an overall rating. This is the process we all use for evaluating real estate; most often, however, we do it subjectively and intuitively without ever really specifying what features we were considering or what weights (i.e., how much relative importance) were given to each feature.

A **weight** is simply a measure of the relative value of a site feature. As related to site evaluation, this means that certain factors and features are more important to some concepts than others. Furthermore, the weight of these features may change depending on the particular situation. For example, as shown in later discussions, it is not surprising that the weight, or relative importance, of drop-in features is greater for convenience concepts than for destination-oriented businesses. The important point to keep in mind is that the weights for each demographic and site feature will vary according to the type of business, the specific situation, and several other factors.

The *InSite* guidelines that appear throughout the book are designed to reinforce this point by calling attention to what factors become most important in particular situations.

CONVENIENCE AND DESTINATION CONCEPTS

One of the most important determinants of the relative weight for a particular feature is the type of business—whether it is a convenience-oriented or a destination-oriented concept. **Convenience** businesses, such as quick-serve restaurants (QSRs), convenience stores, or service stations, depend primarily on a nearby customer base that "drops-in," often for an unplanned visit. Because a convenience business is likely to have competition throughout the market, it is unlikely that you would drive to visit one unless it happens to fit "conveniently" in your daily routine (such as stopping at a regular gas station on your way to or from work).

Destination businesses, such as a particular restaurant or retail shop, discount store, mall, or other retail concept, attract their customers, in part, through their uniqueness. Visits to a destination business are often planned ahead of time and may involve driving ten or more miles, depending on the attractiveness and availability of the concept.

Normally, a business attracts both types of customers—those who planned a visit and those who dropped in because of convenience factors. Therefore, the question of whether a business is a convenience or a destination concept is always a matter of degree. In the site evaluation model presented in Chapter 14, different weights are given for both types of concepts.

CHAPTER 3

PRINCIPLES AND PERSPECTIVES

W hile most site decisions are local (How good is this specific location in this market?), they are also embedded in a larger geographic context depending on the size of your company, the number of markets in which you operate, and your growth plans for a single market. The decision to accept or override a particular site evaluation is often based on this broader context. For example, strategically, you may want a site in the southwestern section of Kansas City as soon as possible and, therefore, may be willing to accept a "B" or "C" location to make this happen. Over the past few years, I have watched with interest as a popular restaurant chain has expanded successfully into many markets using only "B" locations because it represents such a strong destination. For the moment, accepting lower site quality to take advantage of market momentum is an excellent strategic plan. On the other hand, I have also watched sales in a current specialty retail concept with mostly "A" locations gradually decline, creating a serious situation, because of issues not at all related to location.

FOUR PERSPECTIVES ON SITE EVALUATION

While the typical site evaluation is concerned primarily with the immediate problem of evaluating a single piece of real estate for a specific
concept, each evaluation also exists in a broader geographic context. In
our thinking about locations at Tangram, our perspective normally
moves from broad to specific, but not always. Regardless of the order, at
some point in the process, most site decisions will be affected by each of
the following perspectives (see Figure 3-1).

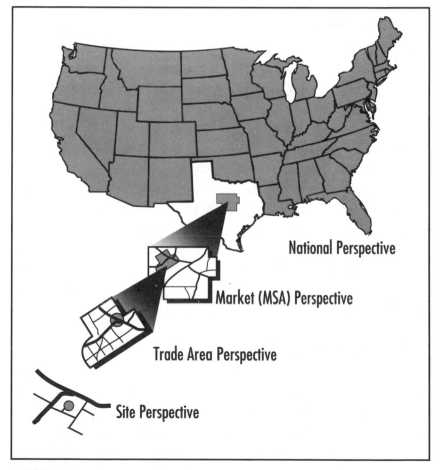

Figure 3-1

Four perspectives of site evaluation

1. NATIONAL/INTERNATIONAL PERSPECTIVE

The decision to be in a particular city or market comes before any specific site decision. Which markets within a nation are most suitable for your business? Do you have criteria for selecting new markets, or is contiguity to existing markets the key? Your need to be in a particular market and the timing around this need may have as much to do with site decisions as the quality of the locations you select. In many cases, the decision is made by default since most business owners begin by opening one or a few stores in the market where they reside.

2. MARKET PERSPECTIVE

A market is defined as the town, city, or metropolitan statistical area (MSA) you are considering. An MSA is perhaps the most commonly used description for a market because it includes a core city (such as Dallas) and all of the associated satellite towns that are effectively part of the city. In this book, the word **market** is generally used to describe either an MSA, or, if the area's population is too small to be classified as an MSA, the town and its surrounding residential neighborhoods.

The market perspective refers to your plan for developing the market. In what section of the city do you want to locate? Where are your customers living and working? Where is the competition located? Are you selecting this site to be the only location in the market, one of five locations, or one of 50? Your need to be in a particular part of the market will probably have some impact on the kinds of sites that are available to you and how much you are willing to compromise on site quality.

3. TRADE AREA PERSPECTIVE

Although there are many different definitions of the term, in this book, the **trade area** refers to the geographic area that contains 70 to 80 percent of your customers. The trade area may take the shape of any polygon, so long as you know where your trade area boundaries lie (see Figure 3-2).

Some site features (such as the impact of competition or strategic position) and demographic features (such as population or the availability of certain types of customers) are actually descriptions of the trade area and depend, in part, on how you define your trade area boundaries.

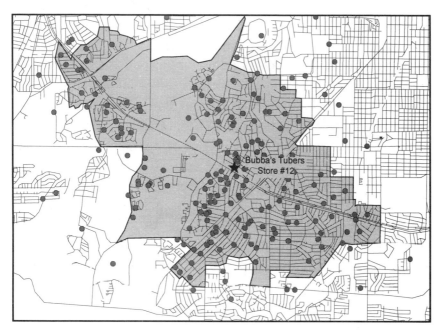

Figure 3-2

Trade area map based on customer origins and destinations. Other approaches use simple rings, block group boundaries, or divide the market into geographically defined sections.

If your concept is destination oriented and you are building only one store, your trade area may actually include most of the market, and traditional trade area boundaries may not be very meaningful. On the other hand, if you have several locations and your business is convenience driven, defining accurate trade area boundaries may be the most critical decision you make in determining site quality.

The site perspective and the trade area perspective are a little like the chicken and the egg—it's hard to tell which comes first. While you often might find a site to consider first and then define the trade area associated with that site, it's just as common to select an approximate trade area that you think contains an adequate customer base and then select a specific site within that trade area. The trade area perspective is presented first only because it represents a broader geographic view.

4. SITE PERSPECTIVE

How good is this location? This book is largely about the factors that determine the quality of a specific site or location and its associated trade area. The site perspective is a decision about a single piece of real estate and includes an evaluation of many site specific features such as visibility, access, type of location, or parking. The trade area is also important to the site perspective because any site evaluation includes a trade area evaluation. For this reason, I will use the term site evaluation to refer to both site features and trade area features.

In a later chapter, I will describe in more detail how market factors and trade area factors can interact with site quality issues in choosing locations. In fact, the context provided by the market perspective may have more to do with the final site decision than site features.

BASIC PRINCIPLES

The ideas about real estate evaluation expressed in this book are based on a set of principles that form the foundation of most of Tangram's work in commercial real estate evaluation and modeling. Time and time again we have found that, despite occasional short-term exceptions, in the long run (over several years), these principles will prove to be correct. Over time, even special cases will be regulated by the same laws that govern more typical locations.

PRINCIPLE 1: SITE EVALUATION IS A SCIENCE, NOT AN ART.

The factors that drive the sales/success of retail businesses or the quality of their locations are for the most part objective and can be measured or studied using scientific tools in order to make intelligent estimates of future potential.

PRINCIPLE 2: THE LOGIC OF THE RETAIL ENVIRONMENT IS DRIVEN BY THE BEHAVIOR OF YOUR CUSTOMERS.

The effects of a good or bad location are determined by the behavior of your customers. Their efforts to locate you, distinguish you from the competition, link visits to you with other activities, come from home or work, select or not select you based on their demographic attributes—all of these factors and more define a logic that describes how the retail environment works for your concept.

PRINCIPLE 3: PREDICTING SALES IS NOT THE SAME AS EVALUATING SITE QUALITY.

The factors that determine the best real estate are related only in part to sales volumes. The old axiom, "location, location, location" is not adequate to explain sales in many markets and retail areas today. This book focuses on helping you find the best site for your concept, recognizing that while site quality contributes to sales, there are many other important factors in sales prediction.

PRINCIPLE 4: EVALUATING RISK AND ESTIMATING SITE QUALITY ARE DIFFERENT PROBLEMS.

The factors that create high risk for a location (meaning there is a good chance that the site will be a *dog*) are only partially related to the factors that determine site quality. You can have a site of average quality with very high risk because of a few specific factors such as very high (or no) competition, poor visibility, or poor strategic position.

PRINCIPLE 5: OBJECTIVITY IN REAL ESTATE EVALUATION DEPENDS ON CONTEXT.

As the introductory chapter illustrates, real estate evaluation takes place within a system that includes several interested parties. Each party has a different reason for liking or disliking the site and therefore uses somewhat different rules for evaluating the site. Objective knowledge about the features that determine the success of a retail location is the heart of an effective evaluation strategy regardless of the perspective. Strategic decisions are strengthened when complemented by a comprehensive understanding of the factors that determine site quality.

PRINCIPLE 6: SITE QUALITY IS AN ENDURING, NOT MOMENTARY CONCEPT.

If your new location has to be an immediate success, the most important considerations for you may have only a little to do with location quality and more to do with image or marketing. A good location does not guarantee good sales or quick success. Over a period of several years, good locations will always prevail over poor locations for a healthy concept. The features that determine good locations or site quality are, for the most part, enduring features that are unlikely to change a year or even several years down the road.

PRINCIPLE 7: INVEST YOUR MONEY IN AN INTELLIGENT SITE EVALUATION PROCESS UP FRONT. DOG SITES ARE VERY EXPENSIVE!

Money spent on customer research, market selection, or site evaluation *before* you build or lease a specific site is *good* money. This one-time expense is small compared to the investment required to open even a single store. Money spent after a site is opened, either to keep it operating despite losses, to change it so as to improve sales, or, most common, to close it after a period of decline, is *bad* money. Now the costs are very large, the period of poor sales may have been long and painful, and the consequences for the integrity of your real estate selection process or even your business (for smaller companies) can be devastating. Dog sites are not fun.

PRINCIPLE 8: DEVELOP A GOOD PROCESS AND GOOD RESULTS WILL FOLLOW.

All too often the only yardstick used to measure the success of the site evaluation process is short-term sales. A new store opens and is doing poorly. Quickly, everyone assumes it is because of a poor location decision. However, this is often a false assumption. First, many factors other than real estate quality will determine sales in any location. Second, these factors vary widely from market to market and site to site. Finally, the largest period of fluctuation and uncertainty for a new location is during the first year after opening.

Short-term sales are rarely a trustworthy indicator of location quality. Instead, your best bet is to focus on developing an objective, systematic process for site evaluation (like the one described in this book), complement it with knowledge about your customers and a strategic plan for market development, and fire away. You may encounter a few bumps, but they will be minor compared to any plan driven by short-term results.

The principles described above are the foundation of this book. My goal for the remaining chapters is to explain how these principles work and why ignoring them puts you at risk.

CHAPTER 4

KNOWING YOUR CUSTOMERS

A critical element in any site evaluation is knowing your customers. Such customer knowledge includes knowing *who your customers are* (demographic characteristics, such as age, income, education, household size, etc.) as well as knowing *how your customers behave* (where they come from, what other activities they combine with a visit to your store or restaurant, what time of day they are likely to visit your business, and how often they use your services). Unfortunately, most site evaluations focus exclusively on demographic attributes, overlooking the wealth of information that a general knowledge of customer behavior can provide. For example, the following are some important behaviors not included in a typical demographic report.

- Frequency of usage
- Distances traveled
- Origins and destinations

- Reasons for coming
- Linkages with other activities
- Proximity to home or work
- Usage of key competitors

Yet, each of these behaviors may have as much impact in determining the success of your business as the more standard demographic characteristics.

CUSTOMER SOURCES

One of the most important determinants of customer behavior is the **customer source**. Where do your customers come from? How many customers will come from each source? Will the total number of customers from all sources reach the required threshold for this site to succeed?

Customer sources are really the nuts and bolts of site evaluation. When you evaluate a site and consider factors such as visibility or access, you are measuring site features likely to impact most or all customer sources. On the other hand, when you count the number of people working in nearby offices, you may be concerned with a single customer source.

The following are the major customer sources that should be considered in any site evaluation.

Residents: People living in the trade area. They may visit your store directly from their home, return home after a visit to your store, or their visit may be linked with some other activity associated with home.

Employees: People employed in the trade area who connect a visit to your store with work. They are coming from work to visit you, returning to work after a visit, or work in the area and have their visit linked to some other activity.

Shoppers: People who are shopping in the area and then come to your store, or who leave your store and continue shopping in the area. Some shoppers obviously overlap with people coming from home or from work.

Enjoyment Seekers: People in the area for movies, theme parks, lakes or other natural attractions, or any other form of entertainment. This category includes both local residents and tourists who might be in the area for entertainment purposes. It also includes individuals who are enjoying some type of informal recreation such as meeting friends or exercising.

Travelers: Individuals in transit through the area who stop because they see your sign and your business fits the needs of a traveler (such as a service station, convenience store, or restaurant), or they are staying overnight in the area and your business is a draw, as a destination or convenience, for them.

Commuters: Commuters are a unique source of business. Going to and from work, they may travel past your location daily, but not live or work in the trade area. This category can also be treated as a special type of traveler.

Special Populations: For some concepts, the presence of a school, military base, or seasonal residents near the site can add a strong customer source that is not adequately described by neighborhood demographics.

Other Customer Sources: Obviously, there are many special customer sources not considered in the above list. These are often the result of special linkages (service station/restaurant combinations) or sites associated with a larger destination (airport or stadium locations, sites inside of a major discounter, special business locations, or school locations). Take-out customers or customers wanting home delivery also represent special sources in some sense.

InSite

Generally, a strong diversified set of customer sources offers higher sales potential and less risk than a strong but limited set of sources. It is possible to have strong sales based on one or two customer sources, but this may also increase the risk.

LINKAGES

From the customer's perspective, a visit to a retail location is usually "linked" to one or more other businesses. For example, shoppers and workers often need a convenient place to dine. Travelers find that convenience store items are now a must with gasoline stops. Grocery or pharmacy shoppers may also want a video store, a bank, a post office, a cleaner, or other businesses nearby. Malls and strip centers were created, in part, to facilitate convenient **linkages**, often between major draws (anchors in malls, major restaurants, or "category killers" in strip centers) and smaller concepts who could benefit from the traffic attracted to a larger draw.

One major development in the retail and restaurant environment today is the purposeful creation of linkages. Most of these alliances are based on one of the following models.

1. Two associated convenience concepts operate out of the same facility (gas and convenience store, gas and quick-serve restaurant, convenience store and video, etc.).

2. One or more convenience concepts are located inside of a destination concept (grocery and food kiosks, quick-serve restaurants and discount chains, etc.).

3. A single business creates special areas that increase draw by providing a linkage option that didn't exist otherwise (McDonald's Playland concept, art display areas, automatic tellers, etc.).

4. Restaurant or retail concepts link with a special destination, such as an airport, college, stadium, or theme park, to provide goods and services.

The major retailers and restaurant chains testing linkages understand their power, yet actually have very little concrete knowledge about which links work and why. Linked errands represent one hallmark of a time-oriented and mobile society. There is a powerful synergy that takes place even in small strip centers when businesses relate in a way that supports the multiple needs of the consumer. When you evaluate a potential site, you will be looking for linkages that are likely to enhance the overall draw of the area without providing too much additional competition.

When evaluating sites at Tangram, we are very concerned with the other places the customer will visit on this trip. The higher the probability of the customer visiting another retail concept during an outing to your store, the more important it is to be in a cluster of businesses containing that concept (unless it's a competitor). As you evaluate the importance of various customer sources to your concept, ask yourself which surrounding businesses create a healthy synergy, especially for customers coming from home, work, or shopping.

 InSite

Look for linked clusters of retail activity that support your business by giving customers more than one reason to be in the area.

DAY PARTS

The fact that your customers dine or shop in patterns that depend on the time of day is another customer behavior that provides an important source of information for site evaluation. Retail businesses, quick-serve restaurants, and other concepts that depend largely on daytime population obviously need to be in areas that provide this customer source. The more convenience oriented the business, the more this is true. Our research shows, for example, that shoppers seldom travel more than one mile between stores or restaurants. Destination-oriented businesses that are large enough to generate their own "gravity" can do well without a large daytime population in the immediate area—for a while. Eventually a competitor will outposition them relative to their customer base and business will decline.

Many very common mistakes in site selection result from misplaced confidence in two seemingly logical beliefs about day parts.

1. The **law of compensation** assumes that slow business in one day part will be "compensated" with strong business in another day part. For example, if a downtown restaurant location does poorly in the evening when office employees have gone home, it will make up for this by having a great lunch business. There is obviously some validity to this law—many successful businesses depend largely on a single day part for their success—but this law becomes problematic when applied to more average locations to justify tough decisions. Only exceptional locations can justify the loss of a normal day part through compensation from increased sales in another day part. Space and staff requirements often provide a natural limitation during your "boom" day parts while there are seldom balancing features on the bottom end.

2. The **great evening fallacy** is one I see repeated a dozen times a year, often more than once by the same client under pressure to open new locations. The basis of the fallacy is very simple. A concept that depends on evening business opens a location in an area that has no evening activity assuming that they will be a draw to attract evening activity. If the concept is a Six Flags, a category killer, a Walmart Supercenter, or the best honky-tonk in town, things may turn out OK. But if not, drop this idea like a hot potato! This is one of the quickest ways to build a dog. In a

crime-sensitive society, low-activity evening areas generally do not feel safe, even when security is present.

 ## InSite

Customer demand during the different day parts should match the normal day part activity percentages for your concept, or you should have a strong reason for making an exception.

FREQUENT AND INFREQUENT USERS

Every business loves its frequent customers regardless of whether "frequent" means five times a week or twice a year. Often real estate decisions are based on being in an area considered to be a pocket of frequent users. Such an area might have affluent young singles or couples for an upscale restaurant, blue-collar families for an auto parts business, or many home offices for a computer or office supercenter. Part of this thinking is sound—frequent customers are an important consideration in selecting real estate—but part is folly: Infrequent customers are usually an even more important consideration.

Can this be true? Are infrequent customers more important than your best users? The answer is a definite yes. Here's why. A location with a strong core of frequent users but few infrequent users is extremely vulnerable to any changes that impact this core group, such as a new competitor, being outpositioned in the market, or cannibalism from one of your existing locations. A strong core of infrequent users, on the other hand, is not so vulnerable; in fact, increased competition may enhance awareness and usage by increasing the area's draw rather than simply dividing up a constant pie.

Many companies base their entire marketing strategy on their appeal to frequent customers because frequent customers *seem* to make up the largest percentage of customers and therefore *seem* to account for the largest proportion of business. Simple math illustrates why this approach can be dangerous.

For example, assume that you conducted a survey of your customers over a five-day period. The results of the survey indicated that 20 percent of the customers surveyed are frequent customers, who average 18 visits per year to your store, and 80 percent are infrequent customers, who average three visits per year. One common mistake made by many businesses and marketing firms is to multiply the percentage in the store (20 percent) times the number of visits per year (18 visits) to gauge the overall impact of frequent customers relative to infrequent. This is a mistake. The actual impact is already contained in the original percentages. If 20 percent of the people in the store are frequent users, 20 percent of the business comes from frequent users. Period. The fact that they are more likely to be in the store (because they visit more often) is already considered in the sampling of customers. The population of frequent users, because they visit many times, is actually much smaller than 20 percent, while the population of infrequent users is actually much larger. Let's examine some actual figures for a convenience/retail company.

Total Number of Customer Visits Per Year = 100,000

User Frequency	Visits Per Year	Number of Visits	Number of Customers
Frequent (20%)	18	20,000	1,111
Infrequent (80%)	3	80,000	26,667

Despite the fact that 20 percent of the customers in the store are frequent users, they represent less than 4 percent of the actual customer population! The other 96 percent is often ignored for the purposes of marketing or site selection.

$$1,111 \div (1,111 + 26,667) = .04$$

One key to finding successful sites is to have a trade area containing a solid core of infrequent users. Our research consistently shows that the base of infrequent users is more critical to sales than frequent users. A business location can fail with adequate support from frequent users when the number of infrequent users is low. You will seldom have a dog, however, with a strong infrequent user base and a few frequent users.

 InSite

The best locations are a convenience stop for your frequent customers and an easy destination for your infrequent users. The latter consideration is usually more important than the former.

Chapter 5

Demand

ustomer sources are a prerequisite for a successful location. If there is not an adequate supply of customers coming from home, work, shopping, or travel, nothing else matters. You will not have a successful location. Surprisingly, with the exception of some small town locations and extremely competitive city locations, the supply of customers is not usually a problem. In most urban and suburban settings there are plenty of potential customers. The problem you face in evaluating and selecting a site for your concept has more to do with demand than with the actual supply. **Demand**, as defined in this book, is the actual volume of customers available for your concept.

Demand is a result of the complex and changing relationship between competition, image, and customer sources. Usually there are plenty of potential customers. Whether or not you get your share depends on *image* and *competition*. **Image** is a broad concept that describes all of the features that influence a customer's perception. Image includes drop-in features such as visibility or access, the physical characteristics of the area around the site, and the market presence (or familiarity) of your concept. **Competition** includes any business a customer thinks of when making a decision to "eat out" or to "buy tires."

Both direct and indirect competitors will impact your site both by providing additional draw (possibly), but also by dividing up the supply of customers from various sources. The interactions between these three elements generates a quantitative measurement of the demand for your store or restaurant. The site evaluation model presented in this book uses a fairly simple formula for quantifying demand.

$$\text{Demand} = \text{Total Customers} \div \text{Competition}$$

The total number of customers refers to the number of customers coming from each source (the total volume of potential customers in the trade area). Clearly, the higher the competition, the more choices each customer will have, which will lower the demand for your concept. Obviously, if the number of potential customers is also high, lots of competition won't matter as much because there will still be many customers available to visit your concept. A good image acts to increase the demand for your concept by increasing the chances that customers will choose you over the competition. We tend to prefer to shop or dine at businesses that are convenient to reach within the trade area, easily located from the street, accessible, established in the market, and so forth.

An objective site evaluation is based on understanding the factors that drive demand for each customer source. Consider these two simple examples:

Customers traveling from home or work to a familiar destination concept will not be strongly influenced by image factors such as visibility or market presence. Because the concept is already a destination, the visit is likely to be planned in advance and they can (or will quickly learn to) locate it. Also, market presence is unlikely to be a concern.

On the other hand, customers coming from shopping or travel who make a spontaneous decision to stop after noticing a sign depend greatly on image and positioning with respect to the competition.

The importance of your concept's image depends on which customer sources drive sales and whether you are a destination- or a convenience-driven business. Customer sources are the fuel that supplies the energy for the retail environment. A store's image determines whether that fire burns brightly or fizzles. Normally good locations have both a healthy supply of customers relative to the amount of competition and an image that attracts those customers through the quality of the physical location and market presence.

The basic description of demand given above provides the framework for organizing the remaining chapters of this book. Part II provides an in-depth look at the three most important *customer sources* (residents, daytime populations, and transients), strategies for measuring the density and impact of each group, and some important points to consider when integrating this information into your final site evaluation. Part III, "Site Features," details strategies for evaluating the important parts of a concept's *image*—including visibility, access, position, quality of surroundings, market presence, retail balance, etc.—while Part IV discusses the important influence of market conditions, most significantly, the *competition* and its relation to the overall market. Part V, "The Site Evaluation," is specifically designed to handle the dynamics or interactions between the information presented in Parts II, III, and IV. Part V also includes an entire chapter providing strategies and guidelines for site selection specific to particular concepts and situations (for example, opening the first location in the market for a destination concept).

Read on. If you have a site to evaluate, it's time to get to work!

Part 2

CUSTOMER SOURCES

CHAPTER 6

RESIDENTIAL SOURCES

The strongest customer source for restaurants and retail concepts is residents living in the surrounding neighborhoods. Their impact can be as little as 20 percent or as great as 80 percent depending on the destination versus convenience dimension of the concept and other factors. On average, 40 to 60 percent of restaurant and retail business depends on customers who live in the surrounding neighborhoods. In addition to coming from home, residents typically also make up a large percentage of the people who are shopping and employed in the trade area. Site evaluation begins with understanding the quantity and quality of the residential customers who surround your location. It will be unusual for you to choose a location that has poor support from residents in the trade area even if other sources (such as daytime population) are excellent.

In order to evaluate the influence of residential sources, as well as other customer souces, we divide the area around each site into three different impact zones—convenience, residential, and destination—and for each zone, consider the factors we know to be most relevant. However, before moving on to a discussion of the three impact zones, we should consider a fourth area, the **retail trade zone**, which describes the retail trade area and business activity around the site. The retail trade zone can be as small as a single strip center or cluster of businesses in which the site is located, or as large as several square miles when the area includes several malls and a large collection of shops and restaurants. Regardless of size, the retail trade zone represents the retail activity area a customer would visit to find your business. Usually, it is the draw of the retail trade zone that attracts your nondestination customers to shop and dine in the area around your site.

While not treated formally as a geographic zone in the sections below, the retail trade zone will be used throughout the book to refer to the restaurant/retail activity area associated with the site.

THE CONVENIENCE ZONE

The first demographic zone to consider is the area within one to two miles of the site. This boundary defines the **convenience zone (CZ)** for your business, the area in which it is very easy and practical to shop or dine at your concept because of its proximity. The one- to two-mile boundary is somewhat arbitrary. It might be less in a densely populated city and greater in a small town setting. Also, the convenience zone tends to be smaller for a convenience concept (about one mile) and larger for a destination concept (about two miles).

Regardless of the typical demographic features of your customers (considered as a group), within the convenience zone, a much broader selection of demographic profiles will be attracted to your business simply because you are there. In evaluating the potential of the convenience zone for your business, you should consider the following factors.

1. **Population:** Generally, a larger population in the convenience zone is better. This is especially true for convenience concepts

such as gas stations, quick-serve restaurants, or convenience stores. It is less true for destination concepts because sales will depend more on people traveling from outside the convenience zone. In fact, for some activities such as dining, people will often resist coming into a dense, congested area. A large residential population can also hurt your business when it is accompanied by a low amount of retail activity in the neighborhood.

2. **Apartments:** In general, apartments are a plus in the convenience zone. Apartments or condominiums provide both high density and a population that is often driven by the need for outside services and convenience. Apartment dwellers tend to be either younger or older than traditional neighborhood profiles. Low-income housing or apartments would not be considered as a positive factor for most concepts.

3. **Demographics:** Do not expect to find your typical demographic profiles in the convenience zone. Instead look for a broad collection of consumers who have disposable income and easy access to your concept. Virtually all consumers in the convenience zone who use your type of products will be your customers.

4. **Frequency:** It is ideal to have a few pockets of frequent customers within the convenience zone. Distance or convenience does matter to a frequent user and even another 100 or 200 users can have a significant impact on sales.

5. **Business:** Businesses, shopping, entertainment, and hotels are all convenience-driven sources of customers. Generally, it is beneficial to have a concentration of business and shopping activity within the convenience zone, but it is also possible to have so much activity that you lose the balance between residential support and business/shopping support.

6. **Access:** Your position within the convenience zone is crucial. If it is difficult or inconvenient for people within this zone to access your

business, the location is probably not a good one. Having major streets in the zone that are uncongested and linked to your location is a plus.

7. **Balance:** If you are a convenience concept, density and position within the convenience zone are your primary concerns. If you are a destination concept, access to your concept through a good system of roads and business activity that provides natural linkages (so the entire zone becomes a draw) are most important.

8. **Drop-in Customers:** Within the convenience zone, a higher proportion of business will be "drop-in" business based on a spontaneous decision to stop. Good visibility, signage, and ease of access encourage spontaneity and are crucial, not to the regulars in this zone who already know where you are located, but to the shoppers and travelers who only visit this zone occasionally or are in transit through the area.

 InSite

In the convenience zone, you should be more concerned with the density of residents rather than their fit to your concept, although pockets of frequent users are a big plus. You are also looking for apartments, offices, and supporting retail activity in the convenience zone that will feed your site because of good streets and adequate traffic flow.

THE RESIDENTIAL ZONE

As the name implies, most customers in the **residential zone (RZ)** are coming to your business from their home, although workers are a strong, secondary customer source for this zone. The residential zone begins at the outside edge of the convenience zone and continues to the outside edge of your trade area. Thus, your trade area and residential zone will normally share the same outside boundary (see Figure 6-1).

As we move from the convenience zone to the residential zone, our focus shifts in several respects. Be sure to consider the following important factors.

1. Customer fit becomes more important and customer density less important. Customer density determines the size of the residential zone, while **customer fit** (meaning how well the people living in the zone fit your customer profile) determines the potential of

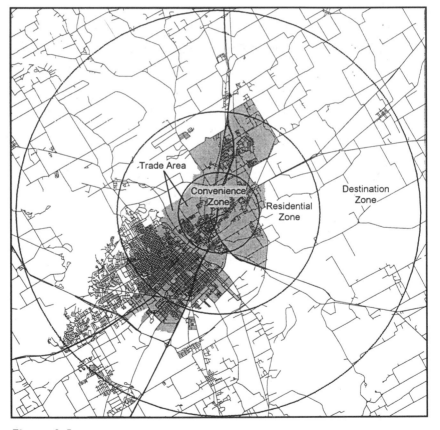

Figure 6-1

Three demographic zones (convenience, residential, destination) and a related trade area. Notice that almost all of the trade area is contained within the first two zones.

that zone to provide demand for your business. In dense areas, the residential zone will typically shrink because of competition and increased drive times. In less dense areas, the residential zone will expand because of reduced traffic and fewer competitive options for customers.

2. The importance of nonresidential customer origins will be reduced. The people who live in the residential zone are the primary customer source. Shoppers fall off dramatically once you leave the convenience zone. Workers will still have some impact, but most will be coming from the convenience zone.

3. Visibility and local accessibility (ingress and egress) will be less important to the people in the residential zone because they already know where you are, and, even as a convenience concept, you are still a "destination" for them. Good signage, however, can help to build market awareness.

4. Because you may no longer be "convenient" to customers in this zone if you are a convenience-driven business, your position relative to the competition will determine if you can attract customers from the residential zone.

5. It is ideal to have a large group of infrequent users and several pockets of frequent users within the residential zone. In evaluating the demographics of this zone, look for both groups.

6. The demographic report is at its best in describing the residential zone because it is usually possible to measure which customer segments are likely to come from their homes to visit your concept. A **customer segment** represents a specific demographic group defined by features such as age, income, household size, occupation, education, or purchasing habits. Actual research on customer segments is very useful in targeting your *frequent users*. Because of their broad base, *infrequent users* are often better described with more general statistics (for example, virtually

every family earning $50,000 or more annually is a consumer at sit-down restaurants).

7. The shift from the convenience zone to the residential zone often reduces the importance of apartments and increases the importance of owner-occupied homes or condominiums. This is not saying that owner-occupied households are necessarily your best source of customers (they may not be, even in the residential zone), but rather that as you move further away from the retail clusters that contain most businesses within a market, you encounter apartments first (because they are often built around retail zones) and then owner-occupied homes.

 InSite

In the residential zone, the fit of the people living in the zone with your concept becomes more important than the number of people in the zone. A strong fit will provide a good source of frequent and infrequent users regardless of other factors. When examining the demographic report, focus on a good fit with the surrounding residents.

THE DESTINATION ZONE

The **destination zone (DZ)** describes the area outside the trade area that provides additional customers for your concept. These additional groups include true destination customers willing to drive a long distance to reach your concept, retail trade zone customers attracted by the restaurant/retail draw of the area around your store, or commuters traveling to and from work. Transients traveling through the market are considered to be convenience-driven customers who don't actually come from any of the zones, but stop near the site based on convenience factors. Demographically, the destination zone is defined as the area between the outermost trade area boundary and the largest demographic ring or polygon used for analysis. In general, we recommend using a three- to ten-mile ring to evaluate this zone's potential, although in some situations, the destination zone will be much larger.

For destination concepts, the destination zone is always important. For convenience concepts, it can have a negligible impact on the one hand, or be the primary source of business on the other hand, depending on the type of location and the number of travelers. Important features of the destination zone to consider are as follows:

1. **Concept Drawing Power and Uniqueness:** If your concept is a strong destination because it is both unique and scarce (not many in the market), the destination zone, which may have up to a 30-mile radius, will be an important source of infrequent users. As the concept becomes less unique and more convenience-oriented, the destination zone will shrink until, for all practical purposes, it vanishes.

2. **Virtual Versus Real Zones:** Any destination zone that is a simple extension of the trade area defines a real area, regardless of the size. Even a 30-mile radius defines a real, measurable geographic area that can be evaluated using demographic analysis. Virtual zones, however, are not measurable. **Virtual zones** are used to describe the origins of customers in transit through the trade area. For an interstate location in Georgia, the entire southeastern United States might be the virtual zone. Although it is possible to analyze interstate origins and destinations, demographic analysis is not usually applied to virtual zones, rather they are simply treated as an independent customer source and their contribution added to the total set of sources. Because they do not have a local geographic origin, customers coming from the virtual zone are treated as convenience customers who stop because they enter the convenience zone and are attracted by signage or other site features.

3. **Directionality:** Destination customers feed into a retail area through a limited set of major roads. Traffic flow on these roads

and the location of good residential pockets along them will
determine the customer potential from each direction in the
market.

4. **Risk:** Depending on customers from the destination zone is
   always risky because sooner or later several competitors will outposition your location. This may not matter if your concept is
   strong and unique and if the surrounding retail area is a powerful
   draw.

5. **Visibility:** Visibility, access, and strategic position within the surrounding retail trade zone are crucial for customers coming from
   the destination zone. Many will be finding you for the first time
   and will depend on signage. Even your true destination customers
   will not be as familiar with the area as nearby customers and will
   depend on access and signage to help locate you. Others who
   already have a general awareness of your concept may drop in
   upon noticing your sign. These factors are most important for a
   convenience business such as a service station or a quick-serve
   restaurant that attracts a large number of travelers.

6. **Demographics:** Customers from the destination zone are customers
   coming from all or a large section of the market. Maps of the

 InSite

The impact of the destination zone depends on the
uniqueness and appeal of your concept as a true "destination," plus good access into the retail trade zone
through a supportive network of streets and highways.
Pay special attention to the drawing power of the retail
trade zone and healthy linkages with nearby businesses to boost your potential for drop-in customers from the
destination zone.

market showing neighborhoods likely to contain your customers are very useful here because you can connect key neighborhoods with the road network that feeds your location.

DEMOGRAPHIC REPORTS

How do you begin to evaluate whether the demographic zones important to your concept contain an adequate supply of residential sources? Enter the demographic services.

For many years, standard demographic reports based on U.S. Census data have provided the basis for evaluating neighborhoods around a location. Summary census data provides a count of the number of people within specific age and income ranges, plus a wide variety of data on education, household size, race, buying power, and hundreds of other statistics. In addition, a variety of trend information, such as population growth, is also available. In fact, more than 1,000 different demographic measures can be ordered by the unsuspecting user of a major demographic supplier! A sample page from a typical demographic report is shown in Figure 6-2 on page 47.

The following are a few of the more standard reports offered by most demographic services and the customer sources they describe.

Traditional Report: Contains information about the people who live in the three rings or geographic zones you have selected.

Daytime Population Report: Contains information about the people who work in the three geographic zones.

Competition Report: Contains information about specific competitors or general types of competitors.

Demand/Shopping Report: Contains information about the level of demand for certain products based on dollars spent or the buying patterns of certain customer groups.

Specific Household Report: Contains information on the location and general demographic/employment/purchasing tendencies of small clusters of three to five households represented by a ZIP +4 designation.

In general, ordering the first two reports will give you most of the demographic information needed for a good site evaluation.

Demographic information is excellent for describing all of the *general* characteristics of the people who live and work in the neighborhood around your site. However, when reading a report, keep in mind that the numbers shown are relative. Therefore, the value of a particular statistic such as the median income or median age of residents in the neighborhood depends a great deal on the context. For example, incomes and ages for good neighborhoods in the midwest will not match good neighborhoods in Washington, D.C. In addition, the compromises made to generate these statistics further confound the problem. Census data is often collected according to census boundaries, such as *census tracts* or *block groups*. The programs used to generate census reports then convert data in the tracts or block groups into rings or some other standard geometric configuration. In order to accomplish this, the program must make a number of assumptions about the data. For example, if the outside boundary for the three-mile ring around your site crosses near the middle of a census tract, the demographic program might assume one half of the people in the tract live inside the ring and one half live outside the ring. However, if the tract were located on the edge of a city, 80 percent of the actual population could live in one half of the census tract. Thus, every step taken away from the raw data to enhance the meaningfulness of the demographic report also reduces the accuracy of the results.

Also keep in mind that census data are collected only once each decade. This becomes especially problematic in new areas where the census data may be older than the neighborhood. The reported demographics for these neighborhoods may show a very small population of

DEMOGRAPHICS

(Summary Report)
by Pete Smith's Census Facts 800-555-1212

DESCRIPTION	2.00 MILE RADIUS	2.00-5.00 MILE RING	5.00-10.00 MILE RING
POPULATION			
2000 PROJECTION	16,814	55,357	78,661
1995 ESTIMATE	15,069	52,378	74,230
1990 CENSUS	14,481	51,426	71,144
1980 CENSUS	13,246	52,383	67,818
GROWTH 1980-1990	8.34%	-1.83%	4.90%
HOUSEHOLDS			
2000 PROJECTION	6,673	21,816	31,712
1995 ESTIMATE	6,212	18,757	29,781
1990 CENSUS	5,764	17,931	28,051
1980 CENSUS	4,852	18,018	25,948
GROWTH 1980-1990	18.79%	-0.48%	8.11%
1995 ESTIMATED POPULATION BY RACE	15,069	52,378	74,230
WHITE	72.81%	55.86%	78.99%
BLACK	18.19%	32.34%	10.68%
ASIAN & PACIFIC ISLANDER	0.52%	1.54%	0.93%
OTHER RACES	8.49%	9.26%	9.60%
1995 ESTIMATED POPULATION	15,069	52,378	74,230
HISPANIC ORIGIN	14.85%	16.60%	17.14%
OCCUPIED UNITS	5,764	17,931	28,051
OWNER OCCUPIED	53.15%	40.12%	61.48%
RENTER OCCUPIED	46.85%	59.88%	38.52%
1990 PERSONS PER HOUSEHOLD	2.61	2.87	2.54
1995 ESTIMATED HH BY INCOME	6,212	18,757	29,781
$150,000+	1.03%	0.50%	2.37%
$100,000 TO $149,000	0.67%	1.09%	2.07%
$75,000 TO $99,999	2.44%	2.20%	4.37%
$50,000 TO $74,999	9.20%	8.67%	14.09%
$35,000 TO $49,999	13.69%	11.47%	17.85%
$25,000 TO $34,999	15.95%	11.85%	16.89%
$15,000 TO $24,999	19.64%	17.06%	17.95%
$5,000 TO $14,999	26.23%	29.14%	19.83%
UNDER $5,000	11.14%	18.03%	4.58%
1995 EST. AVERAGE HH INCOME	$28,689	$25,143	$38,895
1995 EST. MEDIAN HH INCOME	$21,432	$16,664	$29,524
1995 EST. PER CAPITA INCOME	$11,867	$9,740	$16,010

Figure 6-2   Sample page from a demographic report

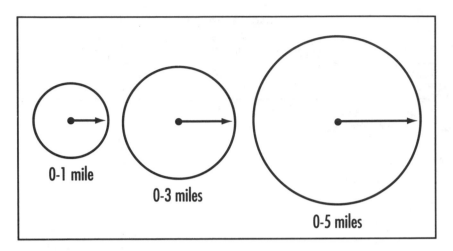

Figure 6-3

Standard three-ring format

residents employed in agriculture whereas the census tract is actually dominated by affluent yuppies. Nevertheless for neighborhood analysis, the demographic report is generally the best available information. Your job is to make the most intelligent use of it.

USING A DEMOGRAPHIC REPORT

The standard three-ring report helps you focus on the details of the immediate area around the site as well as the surrounding areas. Most three-ring reports are based on the format shown in Figure 6-3. Notice two things:

1. The size of the rings is arbitrary. You can order 1-3-5 mile rings, 2-5-10 mile rings, or whatever you want.

2. The rings are inclusive. The point of origin for each ring is 0, which represents the location of your site. Therefore, Ring 2

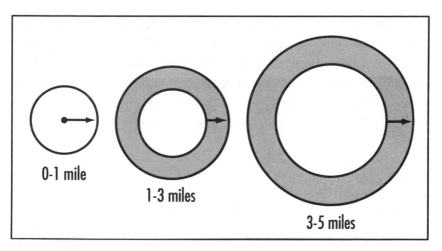

Figure 6-4

Three-ring format with independent zones

contains Ring 1, and Ring 3 contains Rings 1 and 2. Thus, there is considerable overlapping data in the demographic summaries for each ring.

To avoid this redundancy, you can specify the points of origin and the mileage ranges for the two outer rings. In this case, your data will be based on the format shown in Figure 6-4.

· Now each of the three rings describes a unique area. To get the most use out of your report, you should plan for the three rings to correspond with the three impact zones—convenience, residential, and destination.

When ordering your demographic report, select the rings according to the following guidelines.

INNER RING

The inner ring represents your *convenience zone*. Thus, the inner ring usually has a two-mile radius for a destination concept and a one-mile radius for a convenience business. The inner ring is used to describe the population density in the immediate area around the site and, more importantly, to evaluate the site's potential to attract customers coming from shopping and work. Since most shoppers and some workers won't travel more than one mile from their present location to use a store or restaurant, consider this ring to be the boundary of your shopper trade area.

MIDDLE RING

The middle ring, which should correspond to your *residential zone*, normally ranges from one to two miles for convenience concepts and two to five miles for destination concepts. The middle ring describes the number and types of residents who will come from home to visit your business and (in the inner portion of the ring) some of the workers who will be your customers. Usually, the inner ring has lots of shoppers, some workers, and a few residents, while the middle ring contains the majority of your residential customers and some workers. Normally, the middle ring is also used to define the approximate trade area boundaries for the site, so any demographic description of the residential neighborhood around the site will probably come from this ring. In reviewing the demographics for the middle ring, concentrate on age, income, education, and household size to evaluate a fit for your customer base.

OUTER RING

The outer ring, which represents your *destination zone*, may vary in size from three to 30 miles depending on the type of concept and the population density. The purpose of the outer ring is to help you evaluate the total population of potential users. Usually the outer ring contains many infrequent users. Because of the distance, you are a destination to all people in the outer ring. The potential of the outer ring becomes very important in the following three situations.

1. You are locating in a small community and people must travel long distances to reach the commercial center where you are located.

2. The outer ring contains residents who will stop at your business while commuting to work or other locations.

3. The excellent highway system links outer-ring residents to your store. Because of the short travel times, they are actually in your trade area.

CHAPTER 7

DAYTIME POPULATIONS

The second primary source of your customers, the people who shop or work in the vicinity of your store, is referred to as the **daytime population**. This dynamic group of daily migrants fills the streets, shops, restaurants, and offices near your site during the day and then returns home in the evening. Usually there is some overlap between the resident population and the daytime population, but the latter is still a strong, largely independent customer source. The importance of the daytime population to a store can range from nearly 100 percent for urban locations to less than 20 percent for a location in a residential area.

Demographic measures of daytime population may not be as accurate as residential demographics because they are often extrapolations based on a limited set of business or financial data for a market. Nevertheless, daytime estimates are an important and useful source of information for site evaluation. The daytime population can be divided into several different customer sources, each of which needs to be considered separately.

EMPLOYEES

For some businesses, especially restaurants, people employed in the area are the largest customer source. They will shop coming to and from work, at lunch break, after work, and, for take-out or delivery concepts, all day long. Two critical issues for employees are usually convenience and speed (the time it takes to complete a meal or other transaction). Unlike residential customers, who may or may not be driven by convenience, people at work are almost always driven by proximity. Our research shows that for a destination business, most people coming from work will travel less than three miles, while for a convenience business, most will travel less than one mile. For this reason, the effective trade area for employees may be smaller than the residential trade area. In general, we recommend paying the most attention to employees in the convenience zone and then giving some consideration to employees in the residential zone, especially if you are a destination concept.

The demographic services can provide information on the approximate number of people employed in each job category for the daytime population of an area. We have found the demographic distinction between blue- and white-collar jobs to be important as well as the distinction between retail/service jobs versus managers and professionals. In general, high-rise offices bring professionals and administrative support personnel into an area, benefiting most businesses. Factories bring blue-collar employees who tend to dine out less frequently and spend less money, even in convenience businesses. Your task in evaluating the quality of the site is to match the profiles of your customers coming from work with the employment profile of the area.

Many areas have a single large employer nearby rather than a collection of offices or retail businesses. This can be very good—if the employer has policies that make it easy and convenient to trade in the nearby retail areas—or very unfortunate if they do not. Usually a large employer will be a negative factor (even if it provides customers) because it will limit the attractiveness of the area as a draw for customers coming from other sources.

 InSite

Count employment sources within one to three miles that are relevant for your business. Double their impact if your location is a) on a good traffic corridor that connects with the employment sources; b) has good visibility and access; and, c) is positioned well relative to competition in the trade area. Halve their impact if position and visibility are poor.

SHOPPERS

Shoppers are people who have come into the area to shop or dine and have linked this journey with a visit to your business. Shoppers are normally driven by convenience factors, even more than employees. Our research shows that in most cases, shoppers will travel less than one mile to come from another store to your store. A retail area that acts as a powerful draw is obviously a destination and will attract many shoppers, while smaller areas will attract more local and convenience-driven traffic. In general, the more upscale the appeal of the retail activity (for example, a mall with high fashion anchors such as Neiman Marcus, Saks Fifth Avenue, or Marshall Field's), the better the area for shoppers.

There are two approaches to evaluating the potential of shoppers for your site. One option is to rate the degree of retail activity in several key areas such as general retail sales (excluding malls), mall activity, entertainment activity, restaurant activity, and perhaps other specific retail categories. A second option is to examine your demographic report for the number and types of businesses in the area and use this information or direct information on daytime population to rate the shopper potential. We recommend combining the two types of ratings to get the best evaluation.

Once again, there is overlap between residential customers, people employed in the area, and shoppers. As the retail area gets smaller, the opportunity for transient customers declines and your concept becomes more convenience oriented, making shoppers and residents basically the same population.

THE QUESTION OF MALLS

Because large shopping malls are a strong destination in and of themselves, their impact on a retail area will be somewhat different from that of many separate businesses or smaller centers. Usually the "gravity" of a large mall will prevent many mall shoppers from visiting other businesses in the area. In this situation, the position of your business relative to the mall becomes very important. Being positioned on a major road that feeds into the mall is a plus. Being on the edge of the trade area around the mall with limited access and visibility is a big minus.

 ## InSite

Evaluate the retail activity within one mile to estimate the potential of shoppers as a customer source. Consider it a plus if the retail area (considered as a whole) has many shops or a mall that caters to your customers and a minus if this is not true. Position in the trade area is crucial since most of this business is convenience driven even for destination concepts.

ENTERTAINMENT SEEKERS

Entertainment seekers are customers who come into the trade area for entertainment and then link that objective with a visit to your business. Entertainment activities include movies, sporting arenas, theme parks, natural or community draws (such as parks, lakes, zoos, etc.), athletic clubs, and a variety of others.

Links with entertainment activities tend to be direct or indirect. Unlike shopping, where almost every retail or service business can be a link, entertainment activities are supported by a more limited set of businesses. Restaurants, ice cream or other specialty food shops, bars and clubs, or hotels are usually directly linked with entertainment. Other kinds of retail shops, groceries, drug stores, service stations, or car dealerships might be indirect links. I may occasionally window shop in the vicinity of the movie theater before the show begins, but I routinely dine out as a part of my entertainment experience.

Strong draws like a theme park, race track, or sports arena create their own gravity and attract many people to the trade area. Even one of these can make the area around your site an "entertainment area." Weaker draws like a theater multiplex, a miniature golf course, or several nightclubs will usually have only a slight to moderate impact on sales. Position is very important for attracting entertainment seekers because the links with other businesses are usually driven by impulse and determined by convenience factors. A bookstore in the same strip center as a movie theater may receive a tremendous benefit from the linkage, while the same bookstore positioned one block away would receive almost nothing.

Except for special situations where the direct links are very strong (as with the bookstore example above) entertainment activities are a weak to fair source of customers for most businesses. Customers coming from an entertainment activity are usually convenience driven, so evaluate entertainment sources only within one mile of the site.

 InSite

Evaluate the entertainment activity within one mile of the site to estimate the potential of this activity to generate customers. Pay special attention to whether your business links naturally with entertainment activities (such as dining in conjunction with a movie) or whether your site is strategically located to attract drop-in customers before and after the entertainment experience.

OTHER RETAIL LINKAGES

We seldom visit just one shop when we are out. Instead our typical journey may involve a visit to the bank, the post office, the drug store, lunch at a quick-serve restaurant, and then shopping for a new desk lamp, vegetables for dinner, and a video. Research clearly shows that your business is usually supported by many positive linkages and diminished by a few negative linkages. Positive links include most other retail and service businesses with the exception of competition. Negative links may include competition (although some competition is usually a positive), businesses that generate activity that interferes with your concept, or business activity that attracts the wrong crowd of customers. For example, your antique shop would receive little benefit from being sandwiched between a boutique for teenage clothing and a bargain dollar store.

 ## InSite

Look for locations that support your customer's need to link several related activities with a visit to your store. Customer research on the frequency of specific linkages can be very helpful here. Avoid links that will diminish sales through direct competition or a poor fit.

CHAPTER 8

TRANSIENTS

Transients, a third source of customers, are defined as customers who neither live in the area, work in the area, nor shop or run errands in the area, but instead are passing through and elect to stop. Transients make up only a tiny fraction of business for neighborhood locations, but may provide the majority of business for freeway locations. Estimating the impact of transients may be difficult because traffic counts do not separate commuters and travelers from local traffic; however, consideration of the following factors is a good starting point.

COMMUTERS

Commuters are transients who pass your location on a regular basis as they travel to and from work. Commuter traffic is a major source of business for certain types of restaurant and retail activity, including quick-serve and other take-out restaurants, convenience stores, service stations, bars, drug stores, and many other concepts. Position, visibility, and access are the keys to attracting commuter traffic. A position on the going-home side of the road strategically located relative to the competition is usually best. (Coffee, doughnut, and breakfast shops may want to be on the going-to-work side.) Since much commuter business is spontaneous drop-in business, visibility and access are essential for a good commuter site. In fact, without good visibility, it is unlikely that commuters or travelers will have much impact on sales.

How do you know whether or not the traffic on your street (or streets) is commuter traffic? The following guidelines should help.

Local Knowledge: Local retailers or real estate agents will normally be able to answer this question accurately.

Common Sense Evaluation: Streets that are major arteries connecting residential zones with business or office areas usually have considerable commuter traffic.

Traffic Counts: The difference between the traffic volumes at 8:00 A.M., noon, and 5:00 P.M. is a good measure of commuter traffic. If these numbers are approximately constant, there is little commuter traffic.

 InSite

For commuters to have a strong impact, your store must be a concept that attracts commuters; must be located on a commuter traffic artery; must have good visibility and easy access; and must be positioned well relative to the competition or other retail activity in the area.

TRAVELERS

A **traveler** is an individual in transit through the market. If your concept is a quick-serve restaurant, a motel, or a service station with many inter-state or major highway locations, travelers are a major part of your business. Most restaurants and retail stores, however, will never see a traveler. In

InSite

For travelers to have a strong impact, look for intersections with enough retail activity to draw travelers, good linkages with other businesses, good visibility—at least at the entrance point of the retail area—and a strong strategic position.

between are the locations that, because of their proximity to roads that carry travelers, will have some activity from this customer source.

The four keys to attracting travelers are fairly obvious and similar to the guidelines for attracting commuter traffic: Your store must be on a highway that has travelers; must provide a service or product that is needed by travelers; must have the visibility and accessibility needed for travelers to see you from the highway and drive to your location; and must have a good position relative to the competition. A fifth consideration, which is becoming more and more important, is the combination of a minimum amount of draw for the retail trade area and a healthy mix of essential linkages. Travelers are attracted first by the gravity of intersections that have a collection of businesses to serve them (usually several restaurants, service stations, and convenience stores) and second by specific businesses from this collection. Sparse intersections with one service station or one restaurant tend to be limited drop-in locations driven by the traveler's need to stop within a narrow interval of time or distance. Busy intersections with much restaurant and other activity tend to be "destinations" (even if selected spontaneously) that attract travelers over longer intervals of time and distance.

Because the decision is made first to select the intersection and then to select the specific service station or restaurant, good strategic position is essential; otherwise the best positioned concepts will pick off the business. Visibility from the highway is important but may not matter as much as visibility from the entrance point where a traveler comes into the activity area and sees what options are available. In most city locations the same rule applies: You need an intersection that has a collection of businesses that appeal to travelers, good visibility, and good position. Many interstate locations (usually around cities) have no real chance of attracting travelers because they do not meet these conditions. If travelers cannot see you easily from the highway or discover your signage immediately upon entering the retail zone, they may not have much impact on your sales volume.

TOURISTS

Tourists are travelers who stop and spend time in the area. Hotels and motels are the best indicators of potential tourist (as opposed to traveler) business for your concept. People staying in hotels and motels tend to be very convenience driven in selecting restaurants or shopping opportunities. There is also a negative trade off with local residents: Too much business from a group of hotels or motels changes the character of the neighborhood so that local residents are less likely to come. Seasonal considerations may also impact the tourist business. Some areas of the country such as Florida or Arizona experience an annual seasonal migration that can double the local population.

 InSite

Tourists can be a strong customer source in resort areas or regions that have a seasonal migration, such as Florida. Generally the entire area will benefit from tourists. Local tourist impact on a specific site can be measured by the hotels and motels within one mile; however, there may be tradeoffs to consider with neighborhood residents.

Part 3

IMAGE

Chapter 9

Drop-in Features

Drop-in features measure the convenience and potential of the site for attracting customers who make unplanned visits. The visit can be a spur-of-the-moment decision made a few minutes before stopping because the store is conveniently located (for example, you check the gas gauge, see that it is close to empty, and know that you need to stop at the station you regularly use on your way home) or because you see the sign or building and decide to stop. Key drop-in features include visibility, prototype, access, parking, and strategic position.

Drop-in features are most important for convenience concepts, but are also very important for destination concepts, especially in new or highly competitive markets. Good drop-in features can determine as much as 50 percent of the sales volume for some convenience concepts. For destination concepts, we find that roughly 20 percent of the sales volume can be explained by drop-in features. We also commonly find that dog sites have poor drop-in features.

InSite

If a site rates fair or poor on drop-in features, do not consider it unless you have strong reasons for overriding this consideration. (Mall sites, office park sites, and many interior urban locations are some possible exceptions.)

Drop-in features, to a large degree, depend on the traffic arteries that feed the site. The major traffic ways that most affect drop-in features are primary roads, secondary roads, and freeways.

Primary Roads: The primary road is the street that the building facade (and probably most of the signage) is designed to face. In our analysis, the primary road is never a freeway (freeways are considered separately), but may be the access road next to the freeway, the feeder road in a strip center, a normal busy street, or any other type of road that the building fronts. The primary road is defined by the orientation of the building, rather than the amount of traffic it carries.

Secondary Roads: The secondary road, if applicable for the site, is the nearest cross street from which the site, building, or signage is visible. In many cases the secondary road is the primary traffic generator since the site may face a smaller primary road or the interior of a strip center. The secondary road is also never a freeway.

Freeways: Freeways are always considered separately from primary and secondary roads because the dynamics of freeway traffic are quite different from typical business or neighborhood traffic arteries around most retail locations. If the store is visible from the freeway or has convenient access to freeway traffic because it is near an exit, then it is considered a freeway location. Normally, if a site faces the freeway, we will consider the feeder road to be the "primary road" as defined above and also consider the freeway separately.

VISIBILITY

Visibility describes how easy or difficult it is for potential customers to notice your business. Obviously, for new locations, you must make this judgment without the benefit of having the actual signage and building. Visibility is more a question of discrimination than the distance from which one can first see the sign or building. For example, to what degree is your store clearly discriminable from the surrounding stores to a person who has never been to your store and is only moderately familiar with your signs or building prototype? How likely is it that someone driving down the highway will be able to notice you in this location?

The key to good visibility is being able to locate your store and discriminate it from the surroundings *when you are not really looking for it!* Destination users have either been to your location before or will persist in finding it (even when visibility is poor) and therefore will not be strongly affected by site visibility. However, drop-in customers and infrequent or new customers will all depend on the visibility of your store for their visits. When you rate visibility, your rating should be based on the perspective of these latter groups.

THE NEW CAR FALLACY APPLIED TO REAL ESTATE

When you have just purchased or have decided to purchase a particular new car, notice how your perception of other cars changes. Suddenly, you are very aware of other examples of "your car" when you pass them on the street. If your car is a Corvette, you might give special notice to all Corvettes that you pass. Likewise, owning or representing a particular concept changes your perception of that concept. In particular, we find that many people have a tendency to overrate the visibility of their concept because it is actually much more evident to them than to a naive user. You can pick the first hint of your sign's colors or building's shape from a sea of surrounding retail at great distances, while a new customer may need to stumble over the front step to notice it.

Recently, Tangram agreed to help a client do site research and asked for the nearest location of their concept for our preliminary studies.

To our surprise, one was located on a major freeway traveled daily by two members of our staff. Neither had ever noticed the sign! The sign was technically quite visible, but the combination of the lack of familiarity with the concept and the sign's generic look (the sign did not suggest a specific type of business) rendered it virtually invisible to passing motorists. Company staff rated the visibility of this store as good, while to a naive motorist it actually had a poor or fair rating.

PROTOTYPE

A **prototype** is the standard building or signage configuration for your concept. A distinguishable prototype adds to visibility by providing consistent cues about your concept that support the signage. The strongest prototypes have the following features:

1. **Style:** The style of the building and signage should fit the concept. Churches, some types of restaurants, banks, schools, and many businesses have a certain look that is communicated by their signs and building. The better your concept's building or facade fits the expected prototype, the more visible it will be.

2. **Distinctiveness:** The more distinctive the prototype, the easier for your observation of a small part of that prototype to signal that the concept is present. Imagine looking at a wall and seeing just a portion of the bumper and back end of an old Volkswagon peeking from behind it. Most people could still immediately identify the car as a VW bug. Try that with today's collection of homogeneous automobiles. Impossible! Now ask, "How clearly does a small part of my building or sign communicate the whole?" Strong prototypes are distinctive prototypes. For example, McDonald's has a distinctive prototype that is known throughout the world.

3. **Consistency:** We build an image of a prototype through repetition. If your concept is large enough to have many locations that follow

a similar design, people will learn what to expect when they see your business. A particular location will then become more visible to the extent to which the building and signage fits the "typical look" of your other stores. Strip center locations often lack the opportunity to communicate the differences in building style and identity that we have come to expect in freestanding locations.

 ## InSite

Site visibility will improve to the extent that the proposed building is a prototype that fits the type of business, is distinctive, and is consistent with other examples of that specific concept.

ACCESS

The ease or convenience of getting to your store is a measure of its accessibility. **Access** is most commonly defined in terms of the ease or difficulty of **ingress** (coming to the store or its parking area) and **egress** (leaving the store or its parking area) from the major traffic arteries.

A variety of methods and attributes for measuring access are available, including traffic diagrams, traffic volumes, curb cuts, medians, quality of entrances from primary and secondary roads, etc. At Tangram, we generally use three types of ratings for access (often at the same time) with similar results.

1. A detailed chart evaluating ingress and egress from all roads and showing traffic patterns, medians, and other relevant features.

2. Simple subjective ratings of ease of accessibility from the primary road, secondary road, and freeway.

3. Measurements of the time it takes, once the sign or building is noticed, to enter the parking lot, park, and walk to the entrance.

This measurement might be added to the time it takes to leave the store, get into your car, and enter traffic in the most difficult direction.

Which is the preferred measure? I recommend using both the second and the third. The second method is simply the easiest way to collect this data. And, unlike visibility, where subjective measures consistently add useful information over objective measures, there appears to be more similarity between subjective and objective measures of access. Most shoppers understand the meaning of accessibility and could assign accurate ratings of poor, average, or good without any training.

Then, just to check your judgment, I recommend that you also enter your site, park, then exit, returning to the primary traffic artery and driving a short distance, say one-quarter mile. Do this at your peak business period. Last month, I visited a client in Louisville who was complaining about poor sales in a location we visited. "Easy access," he said, as we exited quickly from the primary road and parked in front of the store. "Impossible egress," I said, starting my stop watch as he tried to exit. Ten minutes later we were still caught in gridlocked traffic on a feeder street waiting to enter the main road.

DROP-IN ACCESS

Convenience-driven access is typically referred to as **drop-in access**. The easier and quicker it is to get to your business from the street system, the better the drop-in access. If your business is convenience oriented, drop-in access will have a significant impact on sales. The impact of poor drop-in access on a convenience-oriented business may range from 10 percent (just for being on the wrong side of the road) to 30 percent as construction or ingress/egress problems make access a challenge. Convenience stores, gas stations, quick-serve restaurants, and many other convenience concepts have made a science of defining and measuring drop-in access and constructing sites that rate high on this measure. On the other hand, if your business is destination oriented and has good visibility, poor accessibility will not matter a great deal, perhaps impacting your business only 2 to 5 percent. If they can find you, customers who want to shop at your store will put up with difficult access.

The problem with drop-in access is that, like many site features, its impact on sales depends on its interactions with other variables. In other words, the significance of a *good* or *poor* access rating depends a great deal on several other variables such as visibility, strategic position, competition, and market presence. Good access is critical in a competitive market where site visibility and position within the market are average or worse; on the other hand, if you are a strong destination, have only light to moderate competition, and have excellent visibility, people will scale walls to get to your store.

STRATEGIC ACCESS

Another important measure of accessibility relates directly to a concept's customer sources. **Strategic access** measures the convenience of the store's position in the market relative to key customer sources. Measurements of strategic access depend on four key access categories.

> *Resident Access:* A measure of convenience for residents in the neighborhoods around the site to travel to the site's retail trade zone (or immediate vicinity if the retail trade zone is large). Are there good streets free from gridlock? Are there any major barriers between the pockets of good residential customers and the site?

> *Employee Access:* A measure of the convenience of the immediate trade area to individuals coming from work. Good traffic corridors are essential because of the time constraints of this group.

> *Shopper/Entertainment Access:* A measure of the convenience of the site to nearby malls, entertainment centers or other concentrations of shoppers, diners, or fun-seekers within one mile.

Transient Access: Measures the convenience of the site to major highways used by travelers, hotels and motels, and other sources of transients.

Strategic access is actually a feature of the trade area and its relationship to the retail trade zone near the site, rather than a specific site feature. Strategic access is a reality check on the likelihood of each customer source to actually become shoppers or diners in your business. A demographic analysis can often locate potential customer sources within one or two miles, but it is essential to evaluate the convenience of access that each source has to the area containing your business. Recently, a popular restaurant chain built a new location one mile from a residential area filled with potential customers—a seemingly good start. Unfortunately, the local freeway system made it almost impossible to get to the retail area containing the restaurant. Needless to say, the location was not a success. Locating on the going-home or going-to-work side of the highway is a special case of strategic access that applies both to drop-in and destination business.

Your rating of accessibility and its importance to your concept depends on many factors—drop-in access; the degree to which your business is convenience driven; major customer sources and their access to the retail area containing the site; whether going-home or going-to-work traffic matters for your business; and finally the interactions between all of the above and visibility, position, and market presence. In your final site evaluation, you should include separate ratings for drop-in access and strategic access.

TRAFFIC

Traffic is a measure of the traffic volume on the primary road, secondary roads, and freeways near the site. Traffic is a highly overrated site feature relative to its predictive value in site evaluation. Obviously, if you don't have an adequate traffic volume on the major roads, your business will suffer. The problem is that counting cars says little about the potential of those cars to stop at your store. Usually many of the other measures you will include in a site evaluation will also be, to some degree, measuring traffic. These might include competition, retail activity, entertainment activity, restaurant activity, malls or other major generators, evening activity, offices, daytime or residential population, and so forth. Each type of activity is a traffic generator, and more active areas obviously have more traffic. For this reason, traffic and traffic counts are not included as a separate site feature in the model presented in Chapter 14. If your site depends heavily on commuters or travelers and you are considering a location with little surrounding retail, but a terrific traffic count, the model as presented is likely to underestimate the site quality for your concept.

STRATEGIC POSITION

Strategic position measures how well (or poorly) your site is situated in the immediate retail area relative to other businesses. A good strategic position means much more than high visibility or convenient access. Good position succeeds by making your store more convenient to customers coming into the retail area, while your competition, because of their weaker position, becomes less convenient. How many times have you watched a defensive back in football strive to keep a good inside position on a receiver to block any pass that is thrown? Position matters a great deal because it drives our decisions to use certain businesses over others. A poor position within a retail area reduces your convenience-driven business because many customers will never drive past your store. Good strategic position generates convenience-driven business because, even if your store wasn't the primary purpose of the shopping trip, it can become a secondary stop by virtue of its good position.

 InSite

In a competitive market, get the best position possible relative to the competition. High competition, low image, and poor position, spell DOG!

Having the best strategic position means that potential customers, coming from all major sources, pass your location soon after they enter the retail area. As with the defensive back, selecting a location between the customer source and your competition is a good strategic position. On the other hand, a poor strategic position is one in which your customers reach your competition first or can get to them more conveniently. While many factors ultimately contribute to an unsuccessful business, I have found that selecting a poor strategic position is one of the quickest ways to build a dog. Here are several classic situations you need to avoid.

1. Your store is located off the main street in a strip center with limited visibility, while your competition is on the main drag.

2. Your store is positioned near the edge of the retail area and although you are located on a major road, most traffic coming into the area comes on other streets.

3. You are positioned at the end of a chain of similar stores so that the traffic flowing through the retail area reaches you last.

4. You're in a remote section of the mall, while most of your competition is near one of the major entrances or on the primary traffic corridor.

Because strategic position is so important, it's worth fighting for in a market. If the site has the potential to be strategically positioned over time as the area grows, pay the extra money for it. Look for locations that are difficult for the competition to outposition. Consider sites with poor position only when the population density, normal traffic patterns, or your pull as a destination will guarantee a good supply of customers. Consider them, yes—but choose a poorly positioned site only with great trepidation.

 ## InSite

Keep your priorities in order. First, find the best strategic position available. Next, be sure you have excellent visibility on the primary traffic artery. Finally, go for the best ingress and egress possible.

Chapter 10

The Physical Environment

The physical environment is a description of the physical and contextual features of the area around the site. The physical environment is concerned with factors such as the type of neighborhood, the age or stage of development, the amount of vacant land, and the existence of parks or other factors that enhance or diminish the area's quality. Instead of counting traffic or retail shops, an evaluation of the physical environment might indicate that traffic was not only heavy, but gridlocked, or that the area has many stores and restaurants, but no homes within a mile. (This may sound obvious, but this simple fact is not always easy to determine from a demographic report.) The physical environment makes an important contribution to the image of your business because certain features will encourage or draw people into the area (in the same way that a concentration of retail activity serves as a draw) while other attributes will have a negative influence.

TYPE OF NEIGHBORHOOD

Neighborhood descriptions range from affluent and established, to middle-class homes and condominiums, to apartments and retail, to factories and low-income housing. They also range from old to new, developing to established, static to dynamic, ethnically diverse to segregated, safe to crime ridden, and so forth. The neighborhood creates a context for your site that either enhances, decreases, or has no impact on its image to potential customers. Obviously, there is a great deal of complexity to these descriptions, and the types of neighborhoods that are good or bad for your concept may not be immediately clear. Yet, in the same way that you can apply a subjective filter to rate visibility or access, you can also come up with a very effective common sense rating for the type of neighborhood in which your site is located.

A friend recently described a potential new location for a second store targeting white-collar business professionals and upper-income residents. It was located near the downtown of a major city, proximate to a large cluster of offices, and only two blocks away from an active collection of upscale shops and restaurants. There was no parking, but the street traffic was tremendous, and the demographics showed a substantial number of upscale surrounding residents. Although he had no experience with locations that depend on walk-in traffic, there was clearly an adequate population density, and other similar stores seemed to be very successful.

He built the store. It bombed. For months he struggled to understand why, but he eventually found the answer. Although the site he chose was located only two blocks south of a similar retail area, the street one block north served as a dividing line between the upscale, business district and the beginning of a lower-income neighborhood marked by a series of small, family-run shops and kitchens. Physically, the difference between the two neighborhoods was not immediately obvious, but to potential customers coming from downtown, they represented two very distinct areas for shopping. The pedestrian traffic flow of his targeted customers rarely moved in his direction.

This case is not unusual. Often times, the demographics will tell a very promising story, but common sense about the neighborhood will tell a very different tale. A quick-serve restaurant opens in an area with strong demographics, but the immediate area around the site is low-income housing and related shops. The location bombs because residents won't come into the neighborhood for safety reasons. An elegant boutique opens in a freestanding building with excellent visibility and access, but sandwiched between two car dealerships. A '50s hamburger concept locates in an older neighborhood with many retired couples. An upscale Mexican restaurant opens next to a mall that closes at 6 P.M.

The type of neighborhood you are locating in must at least pass a common sense test relative to the type of business being considered. Demographics tell part of the story, but a quick evaluation of whether the physical character of the neighborhood will hurt, help, or have no impact on your business is just as important. Look for obvious red flags; otherwise, expect at least a reasonable fit between your business and the surrounding neighborhood.

QUALITY OF SURROUNDINGS

High quality retail or residential surroundings are usually a positive draw for most types of businesses, independent of other factors. Perceptions of quality can be influenced by newness, contemporary building designs, expensive materials, landscape architecture, unique functionality, reputation, trees, parks or other natural features, and many other factors. When evaluating the immediate area around the site, add some extra rating points for high quality.

Low quality environments usually have reduced draw unless you have a captive audience. Low-income housing, the traditional factory, streets and yards littered with garbage, the absence of landscaping, the perception of crime, and vacant land all detract from quality. On the other hand, low-income households and the absence of automobiles often create populations that are forced, for lack of choice, to support certain kinds of neighborhood businesses. Some of the highest volume quick-serve restaurants and convenience store units come from such neighborhoods.

RETAIL BALANCE

Our research shows that balanced retail areas—ones that offer a variety of shops, dining, and services—often do better than areas with a limited group of retail outlets. A collection of several auto dealerships, or several grocery stores, or even several hotels and motels may have the same volume of draw as a large set of smaller businesses, but the latter grouping is much more likely to give your concept more customers. As the retail area gets out of balance by leaning toward one type of business or another, the opportunity for meaningful linkages is diminished (linkages permit customers to do several errands on the same trip). For example, our research shows that for restaurants, retail areas dominated by a collection of hotels and motels or by a large mall are generally a poor location. There is a natural resistance to dealing with the extra traffic or congestion when your purpose is simply to dine. For this reason, one of the best strategic locations for restaurants is on the edge of a busy retail area, positioned so as to pick off neighborhood or business traffic first.

GRIDLOCK

Gridlock may be a blessing or a curse. Destination concepts may suffer because too much traffic makes it difficult to enter the area. Convenience concepts may benefit because the generous supply of cars (and the potential customers inside of them) creates constant demand for convenience-driven products and services. Access issues are especially important for this type of convenience location. How many times have you not stopped for gasoline because the station was on the wrong side of a busy street?

EDGE LOCATIONS

An edge location is one near the boundary of a strip center, mall pad, or retail trade zone with vacant land, low-income housing, or other nonsupportive development on the other side of the boundary. Certain edge or boundary locations can be benign or helpful to retail businesses, while others can be very dangerous. One common feature of many dog sites is that they are located near the wrong kind of boundary or edge. Imagine a retail area one mile in diameter. A good edge location would be positioned on the main road that received the majority of traffic entering the area. As discussed in Chapter 9, this type of site actually has an excellent *strategic position* because you reach it before you reach the competition. Its position is dominant relative to the competition.

On the other hand, a poor edge location would be one near the edge of the retail area, on a road that had very little traffic. People visiting the retail area would probably not find this business unless it were a destination. An even worse location would be one near the edge of the retail area, adjacent to vacant land or low-income housing and no street system. This is a common type of location in many newer markets in the southwest where vacant land is gradually converted into shops and homes. Being on the edge not only means your business will be harder to find, but it also means that no convenience-driven traffic will pass by, greatly lowering the potential for drop-in customers and for building general awareness of your concept. Also, the perception of crime will be greater with edge locations near vacant or unfamiliar territory.

Treat negative edge locations as a red flag unless you have strong reasons for overriding the above considerations.

 ## InSite

Demographics only tell part of the story about a neighborhood. Always drive the neighborhood to assess a) whether the physical surroundings are likely to support, or hurt your business; b) whether the nearby businesses create a meaningful cluster of retail activity that makes sense for the neighborhood; c) how much of the neighborhood is undeveloped or vacant; and d) the potential of this site to represent an edge location.

Part 4

MARKET
CONDITIONS

CHAPTER 11

THE MARKET

Regardless of market perceptions or market presence, your goal—to select the best locations in the market for your concept—doesn't change. However, the definition of the best location changes considerably based on how you answer several crucial questions related to the market and your strategy for growth in the market. For this reason, the concept of market is actually pivotal for good site selection and evaluation. The crucial issues concern growth strategy, regional awareness, market penetration, market fit, and prototype. Each of these issues in some way impacts the site decisions you will make either by changing the relative importance of the attributes you will use to evaluate the site, or by changing the growth priorities within the market.

GROWTH STRATEGY

There are two extremes in growth strategies: Build one site within a market and quit, or build enough sites to dominate the market. In reality, most strategies fall somewhere between these two extremes. Your position on this "strategy continuum" impacts real estate decisions in several ways.

1. If you are building one or just a few locations in the market because you have a strong destination concept, your store or stores must be positioned strategically near major highways that link easily with the entire market. These do not have to be dominant locations—if you are a true destination, people will eventually find you, but you must make it possible for a large portion of the market to conveniently get to your stores.

2. If your plan is to build out the market in order to become a dominant concept, you must fight to get strategically positioned stores open first and then fill in trade area gaps as appropriate. Locations on major highways with strong visibility and strategic position serve the dual purpose of building market awareness while also operating as successful units. Many firms become sidetracked with secondary locations and lose good strategic opportunities.

3. If your goal is simply to find one or a few excellent locations as they become available without being concerned about market presence or dominating the competition, the site quality score becomes the most important issue for consideration.

A variety of growth strategies will work fairly well as long as you are selecting high quality locations. Unfortunately, in most competitive markets, excellent locations are in short supply. In such situations, your growth strategy becomes even more important as the decisions you make are more complex and involve many B and C locations in addition to the obvious choices. A good growth strategy keeps you focused on your long-term objectives so that when you make mistakes—and in the short run you will make mistakes—you won't be tempted to sacrifice your long-term plans.

The effectiveness of any growth strategy depends a great deal on other factors, however, such as regional or market awareness.

REGIONAL AWARENESS

For chain concepts, **regional awareness** is a measure of how well you are known outside of your primary markets. A Mexican concept with a dozen locations divided between Houston, Dallas, San Antonio, and Austin will have (if it is successful) strong regional awareness throughout Texas and perhaps even the southwest. This regional awareness is invaluable from a marketing perspective because it immediately makes you a strong destination in contiguous new cities. The question, "Who are you?" has already been answered to a large degree.

Regional awareness also impacts your site decision process. Because you will have instant market presence since people already know of your concept, you can select more secondary, less strategic locations within the market and still do well. It is not so crucial that people in the market drive by your signage every day to build awareness and curiosity—that energy already exists because of your regional presence. Word-of-mouth advertising and a well publicized grand opening will let most customers know that you have arrived. It is crucial, however, that you locate near highways that give many of your customers coming from home or work timely access to your store.

 InSite

The more convenience oriented the concept, the more critical it is to have a strong image in the trade area. For destination-oriented concepts, a weak real estate image can be compensated for by strong regional awareness.

MARKET PENETRATION

Market penetration is a measure of market awareness as opposed to regional awareness, although both are usually closely related. **Market penetration** measures the degree to which your present store locations "penetrate" or exhaust the potential supply of customers. In a market with limited penetration, there will be many gaps or areas that might provide an adequate customer base for a new store. A high degree of market penetration affects your site selection strategy in the following way: All sites within the market for your concept are now convenience locations, regardless of whether you are a destination or a convenience concept. In such instances, trade area analysis and site evaluation should focus on local considerations rather than market issues. Strategic position, the quality of local retail draws, the number of potential customers living in your trade area—all of the factors that help to define local site quality—become the major considerations in evaluating the site. Strong market penetration usually means that a store will reach its full potential quickly, often in less than a year, and that this potential will be determined by local rather than market factors (which are already known before you open the site).

MARKET FIT

Market fit describes the appropriateness of the market for a particular concept. Often, low sales in new markets has little to do with site quality and much to do with common sense about market fit. The most famous last words in this case go something like, "It will do great. There's not another concept like it in the market. I'll have no competition!"

Obviously there may be a reason why you have no competition. When there is a clash between your concept and the values and tastes of the market, one of two things usually happens: You are ignored, and if you survive, it is only after several years of building market awareness; or you may just happen to hit the novelty niche and the market loves you. For some years, Texas cowboys, and Tex-Mex cooking have been hot ideas in many urban centers. On the other hand, classic southern cooking is a hard sell in the midwest, and there is a reason why Maine has few air conditioner shops.

If you have a concept that is very novel to a market or that doesn't fit naturally with the market's culture, here are several possible strategies for site selection:

1. Locate in the retail, entertainment, or dining activity centers of the market where you are likely to find the largest number of people willing to try something new.

2. If a demographic niche exists that supports your concept, locate conveniently to this group. Although bagels are consumed by a broad spectrum of demographic groups today, not too many years ago they were perceived to be a largely Jewish commodity and locating near a Jewish neighborhood was a prerequisite for a successful bagel shop.

3. Go after the 18-29 year olds in the market. Although they are the most critical consumers, they are also the most willing to try new concepts.

If your pockets are deep, perhaps you can ignore this common sense criterion and build wherever you choose. If they are a little on the thin side, however, I would strongly recommend a focus group or other market research to help judge consumer reaction before opening a store.

PROTOTYPE

The prototype, or standard building/signage configuration for your concept, was originally discussed in Chapter 9 as an important drop-in feature. A strong prototype also offers an excellent way to build an identity in a market. Prototypes that are visually appealing and communicate the right message to your customers have a strong impact on sales. Ambiguous prototypes confuse potential clients, force them to decide what message you are sending, and result in lost sales. Most retail concepts have a specific "look" that is associated with that business. We expect pharmacies, gas stations, upscale restaurants, banks, discount chains, and other concepts to have a certain appearance. When they don't, we may not recognize them in time to use them.

Unconsciously, we depend on a certain set of cues to tell us about the nature of a business. We are most comfortable when the cues fit what is expected for that business. A good prototype sends strong cues that communicate your special identity as well as the nature of your business. Imagine that you are driving down the street with your family. It's lunch time and you are looking for a table-serve restaurant like Chili's or TGI Friday's. You pass a number of local table-serve restaurants, but in each case you resist stopping. None of them really has the classic look of a casual theme restaurant with the landscaping, typical building prototype, and awning. None of them sent a strong enough message with the building and signage to communicate what your experience would be inside. Instead, you had to rely on the words given on the sign. Another example of the importance of prototype is typified by a well known restaurant chain, which has consistently done poorly in new markets. Their market research showed that the building style they used communicated the message inexpensive, fast food to their potential customers rather than quality dining.

Prototype becomes an important part of site selection because the type of building you construct or lease and the signage you choose are very much a part of the real estate quality. The stronger the identity you create in support of your concept, the better the location. The following considerations may be helpful in creating a strong prototype:

1. Get the help of a designer or researcher to match perceptions of your signage, facade, or building with the purpose or nature of your business. Be sure you are not sending mixed signals.

2. Create a good prototype for your first location, then stick with it as you grow. You want both uniqueness and a clear identity that fits what customers expect from your type of concept.

3. Site quality depends in part on how closely you can conform to your prototype requirements. Keep this in mind during negotiations.

A FINAL NOTE

Poorly performing sites are a fact of life in the retail and restaurant business. Hopefully, they are a small proportion of the total number of sites, but nevertheless, every company has a few dogs. Who is to blame? Occasionally the problem is that a poor site has been selected, one with below average site features. More typical, though, is the glaring error in common sense that, looking back, seems so obvious that you wonder how it could have ever happened. The western theme restaurant situated one block from Rush Street in Chicago's entertainment district; the boutique on the wrong side of the freeway; the convenience store tucked in a mall that closes at 6:00 P.M.—all of these are errors in common sense.

Most often, however, the problem with a poorly performing store has little or nothing to do with real estate. Instead it is a function of the issues discussed in this chapter combined with a poor marketing strategy. New markets require a coordinated effort between development, strategic planning, and marketing. When the developmental strategy is not understood or is simply based on opening a certain number of units during the year; when there is not genuine strategic planning; when issues such as regional awareness, market fit, or prototype are ignored; when there is not a coordinated marketing strategy in place to fit the expansion strategy—when any of these factors operate, dog sites are a definite possibility.

Chapter 12

Competition

You know how the story goes. Fixing dinner for the family one evening while his wife watches the NBA Championships on TV, Bob discovers that the grubcake that has fallen to the floor into the pile of spilled Parmesan cheese, rosemary, and dishwasher detergent suddenly turns a dark, rich brown and has the consistency of French bread crossed with whale blubber. The family dogs fight over the grubcake until one wins and quickly gobbles it down. (The fact that later that night, the dog turns bright orange and dies is lost in the excitement of Bob's discovery.) One month later the first store, Bob's Gregarious Grubcakes, opens in Philly. It's an instant success. Soon there are franchises all over the country. Grubcakes replace bagels—which replaced muffins, which replaced croissants, which replaced doughnuts—as the hot breakfast item of choice. The orange hue is a disturbing side effect, but no one seems too concerned.

In the beginning, there is no competition. Every store is a success and a strong destination. Without competition to consider, finding real estate is no problem. In fact, it is almost fun. A year later, there are a few competitors who actually help sales by increasing market awareness and draw in hot grubcake zones. But within two years, there are dozens of pretenders, all promising fresher, greasier, more interesting grubcakes. Finding real estate is now very difficult—before the doors on a new store can even open, several competitors are already under construction nearby. Soon after this, the first dogs begin to appear in the system, same store sales begin to drop, and customer complaints about the service, the poor selection, and the side effects surface. Now you are just another chain concept struggling to survive.

Despite the obvious exaggeration, this story is in many ways typical of concept growth in this country. Whether you're the owner of a one-unit company or the site selector for a large chain, you face the same problem: knowing how to evaluate the impact of competition or the absence of competition on sales. In our story, there are roughly three stages of development.

1. Competition either doesn't exist or is so limited that it does not matter.

2. There is moderate competition, but it appears to have a largely positive impact on sales.

3. Competition is excessive and same store sales are flat or decline.

Understanding these three oversimplified stages and how they relate to market dynamics as well as your own growth strategy is essential to getting a true picture of how competition will impact the site you are evaluating.

UNDERSTANDING THE DYNAMICS OF COMPETITION

Competition is a basic concept that we all understand clearly at the supply and demand level. The market has X potential customers or Y potential dollars to spend on your product. This is the pie. Within a particular trade area, the more competition, the smaller your share of the pie. Given this reasoning, your growth strategy is simple. Find good locations in areas with high demand and low competition. No problem, right? Wrong. There is a small problem.

Unless you happen to have a very unique new product such as a Siberian hamburger concept (home of the iceburger) or drive-through formal wear (Bud's Duds for Dudes on the Run) it may be very difficult to find low competition/high demand locations. Your decision is much more likely to revolve around the question of "how much competition is too much"—a complicated question with a complex tradeoff. Up to a point, competition probably increases demand and market presence. There is a synergy that develops when several direct competitors locate in the same area. Driving down the interstate, do you normally select intersections with one service station or several? To complicate this issue further, when you make an interstate highway stop, are you just looking for gasoline, or are you looking for a collection of related businesses—food, convenience items, or even auto parts. The cluster of related businesses, which increases the draw of the immediate trade area, has a direct effect on how much competition is beneficial.

Now add a third factor—image. A site's image is a complex mixture of factors that define the suitability of its physical attributes for attracting customers. Site features that promote a good image include visibility, access, position relative to other retail businesses, quality and newness of the building, and the type of location (e.g., freestanding or strip center). Features of the surrounding area that promote an image include quality of the physical surroundings (high quality can be based on modernness or distinctiveness, as in a historical district), draw of the surrounding businesses, integrity of the cluster of businesses that includes your site, vacant land in the area, or patterns of growth and development.

There are other variables impacting a site's image that are not dependent on the location of the site, but rather on the strength of the concept in this market. The non-real estate factors that drive image include market presence (having two or three locations within a market can generate enormous energy and a broad awareness), marketing, mystique, perceived quality of the product, and timing (having enough of the right product in the right place at the right time).

When you have a strong image, high competition may improve sales. On the other hand, if you have a weak image, either because of real estate factors or low market presence, even moderate competition may be the kiss of death.

 InSite

In competitive markets, the best locations today generally have moderate competition and high demand. Low competition may produce a big success, but it usually increases risk.

The amount of competition, the supporting retail activity, your market presence, and consumer demand all interact with the convenience/destination orientation of your concept.

1. High competition, poor image, and a convenience-driven business is a formula for failure!

2. High demand and a good image usually guarantee success regardless of other factors.

3. Destination concepts with little or no advertising need to find high image locations as they enter new markets.

4. For a convenience-oriented business, poor position in the trade area means that direct competition will have a stronger negative impact.

Figure 12-1 illustrates how some of these factors interrelate.

Before examining the interactions important to any evaluation of competition, it will be useful to discuss several key concepts in more detail.

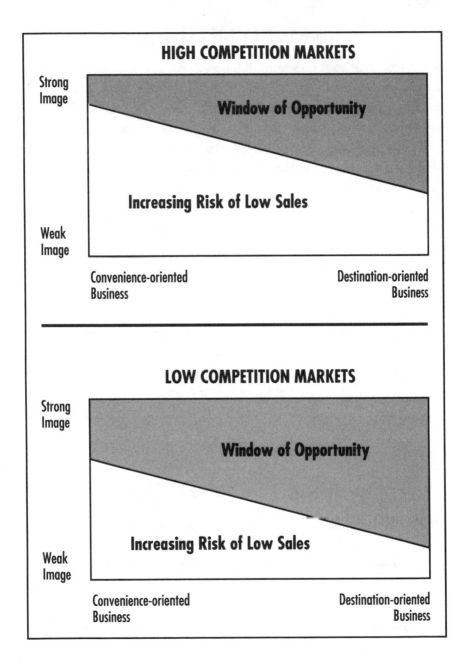

Figure 12-1

How image and competition impact sales for convenience and destination businesses.

DIRECT COMPETITION

Direct competition comes from businesses that are very much like your concept in that their theme, merchandise, food, or target customer is similar to yours. In the example at the beginning of this chapter, another store whose primary sales came from grubcakes would be a direct competitor. True direct competitors tend to *divide* the market, each getting some proportion of the demand within the trade area. Direct competitors are essentially competing for the same dollars within the trade area. The reason you are selected over a direct competitor might include convenience, habit or preference, perceived quality, selection, service, and the *V-factor* (the tendency for people to seek out *variety*, especially in their dining habits and to a lesser degree in merchandise sales and service-related businesses).

 InSite

In a competitive market, get the best position possible relative to direct competitors. High competition, low image, and poor position spell DOG!

INDIRECT COMPETITION

Indirect competition comes from two main sources.

1. Stores that sell your food, merchandise, or service as a small part of their overall business. A grocery store that has a limited selection of office supplies is an indirect competitor for an office supercenter. Walmart is an indirect (as well as direct) competitor for most retail businesses in a small town.

2. Stores that sell goods similar to your store, but with a different theme, price, quality level, or selection. A Chinese restaurant is indirect competition for a casual theme concept. An expensive

dress boutique is indirect competition for a mid-scale clothing chain. The question of direct versus indirect competition is especially complex for merchandise because many retail stores, from discount to specialty, will carry some of the same merchandise.

DISTINGUISHING BETWEEN DIRECT VERSUS INDIRECT COMPETITION

Distinguishing between direct and indirect competitors is often difficult and may depend on the extent to which your concept is destination oriented. Convenience concepts can be impacted by some indirect competitors as much as by direct competitors because the choice being made has a little to do with the brand name of the concept and much to do with the convenience of having that product when you want it. When every supermarket, restaurant, convenience store, bakery, and hair salon suddenly appeared with a yogurt machine, many were strong, direct competitors for the yogurt shops. Destination concepts are not impacted so strongly by indirect competition because part of the appeal is the draw associated with the concept's identity. When I want to dine out and eat steak, Chinese or Greek restaurants—even ones that have steak on the menu—will receive little consideration because they do not fit my perception of a steak place. When I want a tuxedo, a tuxedo specialty shop is a strong destination because I assume that the typical department store will not have as wide a selection or as knowledgeable a sales staff.

Often, your customers are the best source of information when trying to distinguish between direct versus indirect competition. For example, a restaurant might ask customers the following question.

Imagine that you have every restaurant concept in the city located within one block, and today when you came to visit, this restaurant was closed. What other restaurants would you have selected? List your top three choices and estimate the probability of going to each choice.

Collect this information from several hundred customers and you will know who is a direct competitor! Retail concepts could ask a similar question, ask about other merchants visited for comparison purposes, or ask about related purchases during the past three to five years.

CANNIBALISM

For any chain corporation, one of the hottest topics in real estate meetings is the issue of **cannibalism**. If we put a location on Broadway and 7th Street, how much will it *cannibalize* (or impact) our existing location at Broadway and 15th? Most companies have guidelines that are used for the final decision. (For example, *the effects of cannibalism must be not be greater than 7 percent*.) Adding to an already complex issue is the pressure from franchises to keep the impact on their existing stores as low as possible, strategic questions based on your expansion plans in the market, and the general myths associated with cannibalism itself and its overall impact on sales. In general, the following three points provide a good summary of the overall effects of cannibalism.

1. Cannibalism is generally a *positive*, not a negative factor.

2. Cannibalism is more of a *strategic issue* than an issue of sales loss.

3. The impact of cannibalism tends to *diminish* over time.

Cannibalism is considered *positive* because it usually is an indication of market presence or even dominance rather than a poor development strategy. The exception would be the rare situations where you unknowingly wipe out an existing store by opening a new one with a much stronger strategic position. Cannibalism is a *strategic* issue because it is impossible to build out a market without cannibalizing·operating stores. Lower sales are expected in existing stores, as you open new stores and make the gradual transition from a destination to a convenience business. The important issue here is the long-term impact of cannibalism. In general, the effects of cannibalism *diminish* over time. And, even if they do not, in some cases it may be strategically wise to maintain a minimum level of cannibalism to be sure that you are not leaving gaps in the market. From the market perspective, your goal may be to dominate the competition by saturating the market with your store. In such a case, your major concern is not individual store sales so much as the total dollar amount extracted from the market. The same considerations apply even if you are building only two stores in the market.

 ## InSite

For a healthy concept, new customer sources driven more and more by convenience factors will replace destination customers lost through cannibalism.

SALES VOLUME VERSUS PROFITABILITY

Assume your average store needs to gross $2,000,000 a year to break even. You already have one store in the market earning $2,500,000. Now you open a second store that impacts the first store by 20 percent, but grosses $2,000,000. Your total gross income in the market has increased from $2,500,000 to $4,000,000; however, because both stores are earning $2,000,000, neither store is profitable. This is where cannibalism can hurt you the most. Even when the impact is relatively small, cannibalism can diminish profitability while, at the same time, overall market sales are increasing.

 ## InSite

When considering the impact of cannibalism, be certain to frame the discussions in terms of profitability, not overall volume. This may change your mind.

BUSINESS CLUSTERS

One final factor that impacts competition is the nature of the cluster of businesses surrounding your site. The business cluster defines the immediate trade area for your store. The cluster may be the other businesses in a strip center or an outparcel near the center, a loosely aggregated group of businesses surrounding a mall, or another grouping of retail/restaurants that is contiguous or connected in some other way.

Good clusters have two features.

1. **Linkages:** They attract people into the area by providing the options for linkages needed when they visit your store. For example, if you visit the doctor for your fat pills, then reward yourself with a double scoop from the nearby yogurt shop, you strengthen the natural alliance or synergy between these two activities. Businesses in a healthy cluster have a great deal of connectedness or synergy that serves as a powerful draw. Discount stores such as a Super Walmart have attempted to create this synergy by having all linked stores—hardware, florist, grocery, merchandise, electronics, auto, etc.—under one roof.

2. **Low or Beneficial Competition:** There are either no competitors in the cluster or the competitors have a beneficial impact on the center due to draw and balance. Normally, with the exception of restaurants, a retail cluster will have few if any direct competitors. More interesting are the clusters in which competition helps to create a draw.

EVALUATING COMPETITION: FINDING THE BALANCE

As stated many times before, competition is not necessarily a bad thing. The real key is understanding the dynamic force of competition and its interaction with other key variables.

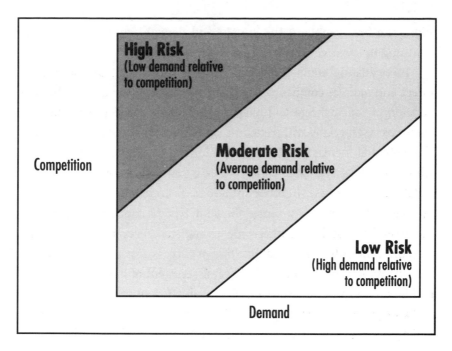

High Risk
(Low demand relative
to competition)

Moderate Risk
(Average demand relative
to competition)

Competition

Low Risk
(High demand relative
to competition)

Demand

Figure 12-2

The impact of competition depends on both the level of competition
and the level of demand.

As shown in Figure 12-2, increasing competition increases the total
draw of the retail area, which in turn increases the number of customers
per store up to a hypothetical threshold. After this point, however, the
benefits of additional draw that come from more competition are lost
because the pie (the number of potential customers for each store) is
shrinking. Stated simply, low to moderate competition helps draw customers into the area, but after a point, additional competitors add little
drawing power while reducing the number of customers per store. Note
that other noncompeting businesses in the area also have a great deal to
do with the drawing power of the area.

Consider the case of Branson, Missouri. From 1985 until 1994,
Branson was a boomtown for restaurants and other retailers. Demand
far exceeded supply. Between 1993 and 1994, however, the total number
of restaurant seats in Branson approximately doubled, and not surpris-

ingly, the breakpoint on the supply and demand curve was reached, resulting in lower volumes for many restaurants.

In evaluating competition, I recommend counting the number of direct and indirect competitors and then evaluating the impact that the addition of your concept will have on the supply and demand curve. In some cases, especially with retailers, one direct competitor is too many. The potential increase in draw from adding a new competitor is small, while the similarity to your concept means you will essentially be halving a static customer base. In other situations, as competition increases, the area becomes known as a center for your type of concept and the draw increases from local, to market-wide, to regional, or even national. Many discount centers have enjoyed this kind of success, especially when linked with vacation or resort traffic. The best assessment of the impact of competition comes from a knowledgeable evaluation of the relevant factors and a subjective judgment of their likely interaction. Here are some general guidelines to follow when evaluating the impact of competition.

1. The retail area has a local demand based on the people who live and work near your store. Is there sufficient local demand to support you and the competition? In a saturated market, any additional competition just reduces sales for all similar stores. In a healthy market, additional competition helps to meet the strong demand.

2. The retail area has some potential to draw or attract people from outside the immediate trade area. If the local trade area is not adequate, does the retail area have sufficient drawing power to support the existing competition plus your concept? If you sum the trade area potential and the expected drawing power outside the trade area, do you have enough potential customers per competitor to be successful?

3. Putting your observations from Item 1 and Item 2 together, what do you think? If you divided the total demand by the total number of competitors would your share be adequate for a profitable store?

What are the volumes like for other direct competitors in the area? If these are below average, the supply/demand curve is most likely on the declining side. Can you tolerate below average sales?

4. In saturated markets with strong competition, two factors are important to consider:

   a) Market Presence: You have a safety net if you are an established concept in the market. New concepts should beware in very competitive locations.

   b) Strategic Position: A strong strategic position is invaluable in highly competitive areas. It is always worth the extra investment after a year or so.

 InSite

To find the best balance between competition and demand, ask yourself the following questions.
1. Will additional competition in this retail area increase the potential draw of the area, or simply pull customers from a fixed base?
2. Are the sales volumes for direct competitors below or above their expected average? Below average volumes suggest a too competitive trade area.

In the final analysis, your job is to make a judgment call on the impact of competition. Statistics on consumer dollars spent per person for your product is a helpful demographic index. Common sense and a little hard information about how well competitors are doing is also very useful. Finally, knowing where this site will be on the supply/demand curve and whether you can tolerate even more competition in the future is also important.

WHEN THERE IS NO COMPETITION

In the example at the beginning of this chapter, no competition was a bonanza. You have a product that's in demand, more customers than you can serve, and no competition. What could be sweeter? Well—maybe. In the case of grubcakes, we assumed they had immediate regional acceptance, so they were in demand wherever a store opened. In your case, if there is no competition, wait just a minute—there may be a reason.

1. You've got a bad idea. Try again.

2. You've got an OK idea that may work locally because of your personal effort or reputation, but has little potential for expansion.

3. You've got an idea that makes lots of sense in Tuscaloosa, Alabama, but there is a darned good reason there is no competition in Minneapolis.

No competition can mean the best of times or the biggest of busts. In any case, it is almost certain to involve some risk. I consider no competition to be a slight plus when your concept is familiar and established and a definite negative when it is relatively untested, either because it is a new concept or you are entering new types of markets. In either case, you should use caution when considering sites with no competition.

 InSite

No competition is definitely a plus if the trade area has at least moderate demand for your product and your concept is successful in other similar markets. No competition is a risk when demand has not been tested or the market is unfamiliar.

Part 5

THE SITE EVALUATION

CHAPTER 13

THE SITE EVALUATION
A STEP-BY-STEP GUIDE

I have covered all of the important issues concerning site evaluation except for one minor topic—evaluating sites. Since this is probably the reason why you purchased the book, let's get to it. This chapter contains a detailed description of the first four steps involved in the site evaluation process. Chapter 14 contains a description of the last three steps.

STEP A: THE QUESTION OF SUBJECTIVITY

Many features connected with a site's image can be rated *objectively* or *subjectively* in a site evaluation. Drop-in features such as visibility or access are a good example. Objective ratings of visibility include a measure of the distance from which the signage or building can be seen as well as the size and number of signs. Objective ratings of access include factors such as the number of roads from which the site can be accessed, the difficulty of ingress and egress, whether or not the roads have dividers, and so forth.

Subjective ratings of visibility or access, on the other hand, involve more arbitrary judgments on the suitability of these (or other) complex attributes. The problem with subjective measures of course is that different raters are likely to give different answers. You rate visibility for a site as *good*, but George (you never trusted George's site evaluations anyway) somehow rates it as *average*. Rather than being a problem for site evaluation, however, we often regard subjective measures as the most valuable data obtained in a site evaluation. Our reasoning is simple. The real judgments of ordinary consumers about the suitability of subjective features (such as visibility or access) determine the success of your business. Therefore, the best measurement tool for rating how a typical shopper will evaluate many critical site features is another person. For example, research shows that the actual distance the signage of a retail store can be seen (an objective rating) has only a little to do with the overall visibility ratings of that store to consumers. Greater distance helps, but it is far more important for the signage to be discriminable in the context of the surrounding businesses and for the site's position relative to those businesses to be good.

Differences in ratings are not as significant a problem as you might think. Most of the time, raters can agree on three major classes of ratings—*below average, average,* and *above average*. We can improve this scale by adding two more categories on the extreme ends. The result is the simple five-choice rating scale used in the site evaluation instrument introduced in the next chapter. Either the three- or the five-choice scale will work well for most raters in the field. In our experiments, even when a group of raters complains about the subjectivity, most give the same ratings on key site features.

Objectivity and subjectivity go hand in hand. Subjective judgments will improve in accuracy as the scales become more objective in their descriptions so that different raters will give the same interpretations to the scale categories. Subjectivity is important because our sensory/perceptual systems are the best yardsticks for judging how other people will respond to a given situation. When using subjective scales to evaluate a site, relax and use your common sense. Recognize that most raters have a tendency to exaggerate in the positive direction when they are actually interested in a location. To counter this, I recommend that you keep your judgments on the conservative side and, if possible, ask the opinion of a colleague when in doubt about a rating. Remember, good subjective judgments are the key to an accurate site evaluation.

 InSite

While a rater with considerable experience in real estate may do best on complex questions regarding retail activity or trade area demand, a naive user, who represents your typical customer, may give the most valid assessment of convenience site features, such as visibility or access.

STEP B: BEFORE THE EVALUATION

Before you begin the formal site evaluation, you will need some of the standard information described in previous chapters. It's helpful to review your notes on this material before you begin the actual process, paying extra attention to the following details:

1. **A Strategic Plan:** This is not trivial. The day-to-day pressures of "doing deals," because your livelihood depends on the number of suitable locations you find, combined with the shortage of good real estate in many markets, can cause you to stretch the boundaries of acceptability. Your strategic plan is a vision that provides the true basis for a bottom line when tough decisions need to be made. Stick to it.

At a recent meeting of real estate professionals, I participated in a round table discussion of real estate strategy. One member of the group remarked that the sites he selected during the last three months of the year were often not as good as the sites selected earlier in the year. His performance was based on a quota system, so he was always struggling to "make his number" by December 31 and would therefore be forced to recommend some lower quality sites. Even more surprising was the fact that his performance evaluation was based on the quantity rather than the quality of the locations selected! Several other participants expressed the same feelings—that quotas often replace a genuine strategic plan and the consequences may be increased risk of dog locations.

2. **Customer Knowledge:** At the very least, some data on the demographics of your customers is needed. Who are they? What are their typical ages, incomes, household sizes, and so forth? You may have this knowledge from direct research on your customers (the best source), comment cards in your store (next best), observations you have made (OK if you will use some guidelines to be objective), or, in the case of a new concept, judgments about the most likely customer base.

3. **Market Knowledge:** What's happening in this market? Is it economically healthy? Is there a demand for the goods or services offered by your concept? Does the market contain enough of your customers for your concept to be successful? Are there other successful examples of your concept in the market? If it's a new market, what level of acceptance do you expect? What level of awareness of your concept exists in the market?

4. **Trade Area Knowledge:** What was your basis for selecting this trade area? Were there strategic considerations involved or was there a high concentration of potential customers? What are the trade area's boundaries—can you estimate these from customer knowledge or traffic patterns? Who lives and works in the trade

area? A standard three-ring demographic report for the neighbor-hood, including data on daytime population, is a good start. Even if the trade area has an irregular shape, most of the time, a demographic "ring" will do an adequate job of describing it. The population of the area may change as you draw an irregular boundary but the description of the area (average income, ages, etc.) usually won't change much.

5. **Site Specific Knowledge:** Have you done the necessary field work to collect information on visibility, access, and other site features? Are there other related businesses nearby that will share volume data or other useful information for benchmarking? How much competition is there? If there are no competitors, why? Did you notice barriers or other unique features that might effect sales?

STEP C: DRIVE THE TRADE AREA

I know, you've already driven the trade area—otherwise you wouldn't be looking at this site—but just this once, drive it again. Start with a map of the trade area, ideally about the size of a sheet of letter or legal paper, a tablet for notes, and perhaps a cassette recorder. (The recorder is not nec-essary, but it can come in handy for noting details when traffic is heavy.)

You will use the information collected at this stage in the worksheet shown in Step D. In addition to being a good resource that will save time at later real estate meetings, keeping good records now may help in other site evaluations in the future and could lay the groundwork for training future employees or developing company specific site evalua-tion guidelines.

Plan your route and then drive with the following issues in mind:

1. **Traffic:** What's the traffic like on the main roads around the site? If it's moderate to heavy, fine, but if it is gridlocked or too light, you may have a problem.

2. **Customer Sources:** Look for your potential sources of customers. Later you will corroborate what you observe with a demographic report, but demographics can sometimes be misleading. Ask two questions about each customer source. How many potential customers are available? How likely are they to come to my store?

Residential Customers: Are there homes or apartments likely to contain your customers? About the only evaluations you can make in a quick drive-by are the type of home (single unit, condominium, or apartment) and the degree of affluence of the neighborhood, but for many destination concepts, this information is quite helpful.

Work Customers: Are there businesses in the area that employ your potential customers? Upscale stores and restaurants usually require white-collar occupations. Retail stores typically have few executives and many service personnel. Also, work customers won't travel as far as customers coming from home, so you may want to discount work sources near the outside edge of the trade area.

Shopping Customers: The number of shoppers in the area is directly related to the amount of retail activity and the quality of this activity. Larger, high quality retail centers provide greater draw to bring shoppers into the area. As you examine retail areas that might provide potential customers, remember that shoppers are extremely convenience driven. Consider only shopping sources within one mile who have a logical (such as on the major road), easy access to your site.

Transient Customers: Consider transient customers only if the site is on or near a road that attracts travelers or commuter traffic. Obviously, for travelers to help your sales, you must have a concept that attracts travelers and it must be convenient for travelers to see your sign, exit, and then get to your store. Much of the same logic will apply to commuters. Do you have a product or service of interest to commuters? Would commuters be most likely to stop in the morning or the afternoon? This will determine which side of the street you consider most valuable. How are you strategically positioned relative to any direct competition? Being outpositioned along a major highway can eliminate most travel business.

A Simple Strategy for Driving the Trade Area

Let's assume your trade area has approximately a two-mile radius. Drive the major roads that feed the site for approximately two miles in each direction, forming a simple cross shape (+) in a typical market with perpendicular streets. Now, on each leg of the cross, 1 to $1^1/2$ miles from the site, drive about a mile into the neighborhoods on the left and right. Look for a major feeder street, if it exists, to take you back into the neighborhood. As the streets become less regular because of barriers, hills, or zoning, adjust your route accordingly. Remember, to your customer the critical factor is time, not distance: Thus, when traffic flows easily and rapidly along a major street or freeway you may want to stretch the two-mile distance; when it is congested or slow moving, you should reduce the distance traveled.

---

3. **Competition:** Look for competition and mark any direct competitors on your map. Depending on your business you may want to mark indirect competitors as well—but for a convenience store or quick-serve restaurant, this number can become large, quickly. Pay special attention to the position of the competition relative to your site. If you and several competitors are clustered together (such as in a restaurant row), position within the cluster may not matter, but position on the main streets relative to your competitors

will always matter. Also, if the area is still developing, be watching for the competitors who are not there. What's the chance of being outpositioned later?

4. **Study the Physical Attributes of the Neighborhood:**

Age: How old is the neighborhood? Is the age likely to matter to your concept? Many companies thrive by becoming destinations for residents in older neighborhoods. Others find older neighborhoods with little retail problematic because they do not attract shoppers and employees.

Decline: More important than age is the pattern of development in the neighborhood. Is it declining, maintaining status quo, or improving? New construction and renovation send a strong message about improvements. Vacant houses, limited landscaping, and marginal retail operations speak to decline.

Crime: Does the area around this location have a reputation for high crime rates?

Vacant Land and Edge Sites: A large area of vacant land near the site generally reduces site quality. This is especially true if the site is adjacent to the vacant land and is perceived to be too isolated with little surrounding activity after dark. I know of more than one concept that doubled their sales by moving from the dead end of a large strip center to the active end.

Ethnicity: Is there an obvious ethnic boundary within the trade area? In some cases, such a boundary can create a de facto barrier because of the perception of cultural or language differences.

Low-income Housing: With the exception of concepts targeting low-income families, a block of low-income housing near the site probably reduces the quality of the location.

Natural Amenities: Notice parks, landscaping, trees, and other natural amenities as you drive. If they enhance the perceived quality of the area around the site or provide additional draw, they will be beneficial to you. However, parks can also attract crime and represent vacant land to a potential customer.

5. **Evaluate Drop-in Features From A Customer's Perspective:** Drive by the site and imagine the signage and building prototype that your plans and zoning will allow. How distinct will the building and surroundings be when compared to your competition and other nearby retail stores? Also, if possible, test the access from the street or streets near the site. Is the traffic you are experiencing typical?

6. **Examine the Activity Around the Site Retail Activity:** Look for strip centers, power centers, business clusters, malls, and local business activity.

   Entertainment: Look for a theater multiplex, large or small entertainment parks, athletic clubs, sports stadiums, and other possible sources of entertainment activity.

   Offices: Look for an office complex or a collection of professional or other office clusters. Large companies may or may not provide office traffic depending on whether they have a dining room or other policies that encourage employees to stay at the facility.

   Schools: Schools can be an asset or liability depending on the school and the type of business. Convenience concepts need to be close to the school (preferably next door), while destination concepts need to be within one to two miles.

7. **Consider the Intangibles:** What's missing? Do several of your neighboring stores have security guards? If so, that might be a strong statement about potential crime. How well are the other

businesses near the site doing? Are they busy and obviously prosperous or is it hard to tell? A few minutes in conversation with local retailers can be very revealing. People like to share information if you will let them. Is there construction in the area to be considered? Has any business closed recently?

STEP D: STUDY THE DEMOGRAPHICS

Now the demographic report is more than numbers. You've driven the neighborhood. Do the demographics match your experience? If they don't, either you have missed key pockets of residents or businesses or the report is out of date (not likely except in very new neighborhoods). Demographics give a good description of the people who live and work in the trade area. As you study your demographic report, focus on two key issues: 1) Are there enough residents and employees? and 2) Do they fit your concept? (See pages 47-51 for more detailed information on using demographic reports.)

1. **Population (Are there enough people?):**

   Residents: Because the number of competitors usually increases as the population in the trade area increases, an absolute measure such as the total population or total number of households is often not a good indicator of the actual population that represents your share of the demand in the trade area. As a simple guide, I recommend that you study several of your stores (or a competitor's stores) that are doing well and compute the following ratio:

Market Share = Population in Trade Area ÷ Number of Direct Competitors

   This gives a rough measure of how many people per direct competitor are needed to have a successful store (recognizing that there are many other factors operating here). The same formula can be cautiously applied to new locations as a very rough check on the adequacy of the population.

Employees: Daytime population statistics will tell you how many people work within one to two miles of the site. Combine this data with the employee fit information provided in Item #2 (Customer Fit) to evaluate the potential of the daytime population to provide a reliable customer source.

2. **Customer Fit (Do the right people live and work in the neighborhood?):**

Neighborhood Fit: A large population of nonusers will do little for your sales, but a small group of dedicated frequent users combined with a healthy supply of infrequent users will keep you smiling and in the black. What do the demographics say? How many of the people living or working in the neighborhood are your clients? Use the age, income, and household size portions of the report for your evaluation. Even better, if your customers have been classified into highly specific demographic groups or segments, you may have more precise information on where they live or how frequently they use your product.

Employee Fit: To evaluate employee fit, I recommend dividing the employment categories by industry into rough white- and blue-collar segments. This allows you to determine how many of each group will be in the neighborhood around the site to give you an evaluation of this customer source.

Much of what can be learned from demographics boils down to two simple equations:

Employee Potential = Employee Population x Employee Fit

Resident Potential = Resident Population x Resident Fit

Chapter 14

Using the Site Evaluation Model

A Step-by-step Guide

You have collected data on site features, a demographic report, the physical attributes of the neighborhood, competition, special conditions that impact the site, and many other facts. You have driven the neighborhood at least once. You have reviewed your strategic plan and information on the market and determined that this site fits the basic principles of your development strategy and that this market is appropriate for your concept. All that remains is to combine the information for a final site evaluation score.

STEP E: ENTERING DATA IN THE MODEL WORKSHEET

A simple model worksheet for calculating a site score is shown on pages 115-117. A similar model worksheet and computer program for evaluating site quality is available on a piece of software developed by Tangram Corporation. (See software kit order form at the front of the book.) The software version of the model automatically attributes the appropriate weights for each possible response based on whether the concept is a convenience or destination business and which of the three demographic zones is under consideration.

Now you can begin entering the information you have collected into the worksheet. For most entries, you will be choosing a number on a scale of 1 to 5 (with 5 being the highest score and 1 being the lowest) to rate the potential of each factor to impact your business. Note that for some entries, you will actually need to first enter separate scores for the relevant zones—convenience (CZ), residential (RZ), and destination (DZ)—before calculating the final score for that category. In order to do this, you will need to first determine the approximate size of each zone. Ideally, the size of the zones will be consistent with the rings displayed on your demographic report. If you have an irregular trade area, this will be less true, and you may want to consider ordering a special demographic report based on the actual trade area boundaries. Under typical circumstances, the following breakdown should be appropriate for most concepts. (See Chapter 6 for more information on determining zone size and demographic rings.)

	Convenience Concept	Destination Concept
Convenience Zone	0-1 miles	0-2 miles
Residential Zone	1-2 miles	2-5 miles
Destination Zone	2-5 miles	5-10 miles

Enter the information on zone sizes in the appropriate box at the top of the worksheet. It will be important to have as a part of the final site evaluation report. (Instructions for completing the worksheet are continued on page 118.)

SITE EVALUATION WORKSHEET

Demographic Zones

Convenience Zone (C Z) ___ – ___ miles

Residential Zone   (R Z) ___ – ___ miles

Destination Zone   (D Z) ___ – ___ miles

Site Information

Site #: _____

Address: _____

City, State: _____

I. RESIDENT POPULATION

	C Z __ % for concept	R Z __ % for concept	D Z __ % for concept	Final Score
A. Neighborhood Population	__ x __ %	+ __ x __ %	+ __ x __ % →	
B. Special Population	__ x __ %	+ __ x __ %	+ __ x __ % →	
C. Resident Fit	__ x __ %	+ __ x __ %	+ __ x __ % →	

	C Z	R Z	D Z
Age			
Income			
Education			
Household Size			
Buying Power			

II. DAY PART POPULATION

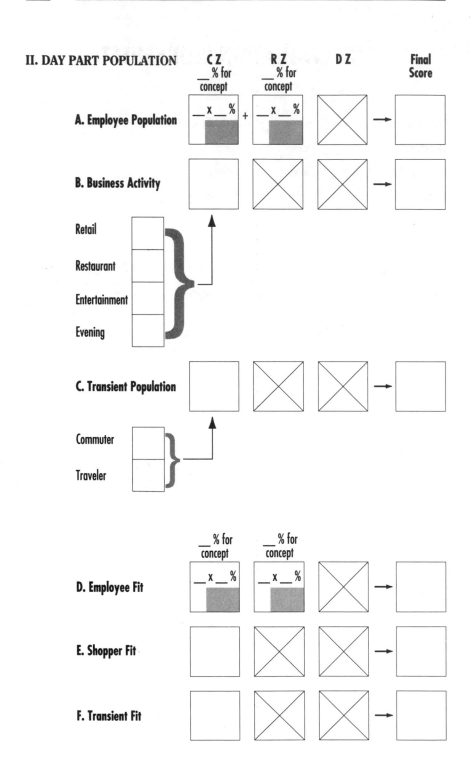

III. COMPETITION

Final Score

Subtotal for Demand

A. Demand Rating

B. Competition

Direct

Indirect

C. Cannibalism

IV. SITE FEATURES

Visibility

Prototype

Access

Strategic Position

Parking

A. Drop-In Features

Surroundings

Growth

Resident Access

Employee Access

Business Cluster

B. Trade Area Features

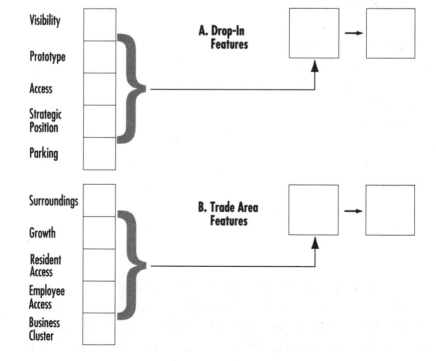

I. RESIDENT POPULATION

The site evaluation worksheet starts by assessing the impact of the resident population, including both neighborhood and special populations and the fit or the appropriateness of these populations to your concept.

The first step is to estimate what percent of your customers will come from each of the three zones. As a basic rule of thumb, I suggest the following breakdown for convenience and destination concepts. You may choose different percentages, however, based on your own experience, as long as the percentages for the three zones add up to 100.

Convenience Concepts		**Destination Concepts**	
Convenience Zone	60%	Convenience Zone	30%
Residential Zone	30%	Residential Zone	40%
Destination Zone	10%	Destination Zone	30%

Enter this number in the "__ % for concept" line immediately above each of the three zone columns.

A. Neighborhood Population

Based on an examination of area demographics, use the following scale to rate the volume of the resident population available to your concept in each of the three zones. (Note that you must enter a separate rating for each zone.)

5 Abundant
4 Good
3 Adequate
2 Fair
1 Sparse

Now multiply each of the three ratings by the respective number entered as the ___% for concept at the top of each column (see Example 1, page 119). Be sure to multiply by the percentage (rather than the whole number), or to convert the percentage to a decimal (for example,

50% would become .50). The resulting number is the final neighborhood population rating for that zone. Enter this number in the shaded box in the lower right corner of each cell. The final score for neighborhood population is determined by adding together the final ratings for all three zones. The resulting number should be between 1 and 5. Enter this number in the appropriate box.

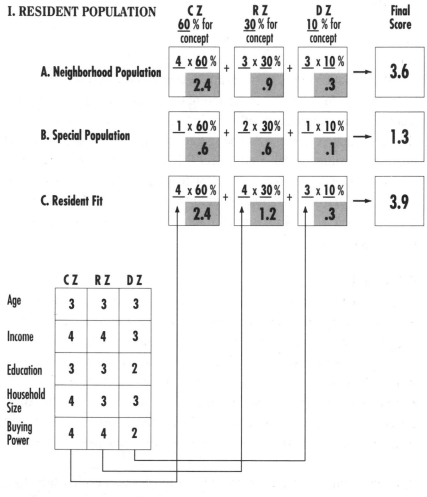

Example 1

Sample worksheet for resident population for a convenience concept.

B. Special Populations

Use the following scale to rate the volume of special populations (e.g., military base, college, seasonal/resort) available to your concept in each of the three zones.

5 Abundant

4 Good

3 Adequate

2 Fair

1 Sparse

Multiply each of the three ratings by the respective number entered as the " __ % for concept" at the top of each column. Again, be sure to multiply by the percentage rather than the whole number, or to convert the percentage to a decimal. The resulting number is the final special population rating for that zone. Enter this number in the shaded box in the lower right corner of each cell. The final score for the impact of special populations is determined by adding together the final ratings for all three zones. The resulting number should be between 1 and 5. Enter this number in the appropriate box.

C. Resident Fit

To evaluate resident fit, you will be rating the portion of residents in each zone that fit your customer profile. In order to best evaluate resident fit, it helps to first assess the individual factors (age, income, education, household size, and buying power) that will contribute to your rating. Your first step is to select a rating for each of these five categories. (Note that you must also enter a rating for each of the three zones.) Your ratings should be based on information found in your demographic report, as well as your own evaluation of the trade area.

Age: What portion of each zone is likely to contain people whose ages are like the ages of your customers?

5 All

4 Most

3 Some
2 A little
1 None

Income: What portion of each zone is likely to contain people whose incomes are like the incomes of your customers?

5 All
4 Most
3 Some
2 A few
1 None

Education: What portion of each zone is likely to contain people whose education level is like the education level of your customers?

5 All
4 Most
3 Some
2 A few
1 None

Household Size: What portion of each zone is likely to contain people whose household size is like the household size of your customers?

5 All
4 Most
3 Some
2 A few
1 None

Buying Power: What portion of each zone is likely to contain people whose buying power represents sufficient disposable income to purchase your products or services?

5 All
4 Most
3 Some
2 A few
1 None

Now you are ready to enter a final resident fit rating for each of the three zones. You should base this evaluation on the ratings entered for each of the five individual categories (age, income, education, household size, and buying power); however, it may be best to avoid simply averaging the scores found in the individual categories. Instead, use your own judgment to determine which of the resident fit categories are most important to your concept. For example, if experience tells you that buying power and income are more important in determining your customer base than household size or age, you should slant your final rating to reflect their relative importance.

With this in mind, use the scale below to rate the portion of residents in each zone that fit your customer profile.

5 All
4 Most
3 Some
2 A few
1 None

Multiply each of the three ratings by the respective number entered as "__ % for concept" at the top of the page (see Example 1, page 119). The resulting number is the final resident fit rating for that zone. Enter this number in the shaded box in the lower right corner of each cell. The final score for resident fit is determined by adding together the final ratings for all three zones. The resulting resident fit score should be between 1 and 5. Enter this number in the appropriate box.

II. Day Part Population

This section of the site evaluation worksheet assesses the impact of non-resident populations, such as employees, shoppers, and transients.

A. Employee Population

The first step in determining the impact of employee populations is to estimate what percentage of employees using your concept will be found in the first two zones (convenience and residential). As discussed in

Chapter 7, the convenience zone usually provides the primary source of employees. Although a few employees may travel from the close side of the residential zone, its impact will be significantly less than the convenience zone. Because it is very unlikely that employees will travel more than a few miles to reach your business, the destination zone is not included in this score. Although you may revise these numbers based on your own experience, I suggest the following breakdown for both convenience and destination concepts.

Convenience Zone 70%

Residential Zone   30%

Enter this number in the "__ % for concept" line above the convenience and residential zone columns. The two numbers added together must total 100.

Now, based on an examination of area demographics and your evaluation of the trade area, use the scale below to rate the volume of employees available to your concept in each of the three zones.

5 Abundant

4 Good

3 Adequate

2 Fair

1 Sparse

Multiply both ratings by the respective number entered as " __% for concept" (see Example 2, page 124). The resulting number is the final employee population rating for that zone. Enter this number in the shaded box in the lower right corner of each cell. The final score for employee population is determined by adding together the final ratings for both zones. The resulting employee population score should be between 1 and 5. Enter this number in the appropriate box.

B. Business Activity

To evaluate business activity, you will be rating the level of overall activity in the retail trade area around your proposed site.

II. DAY PART POPULATION

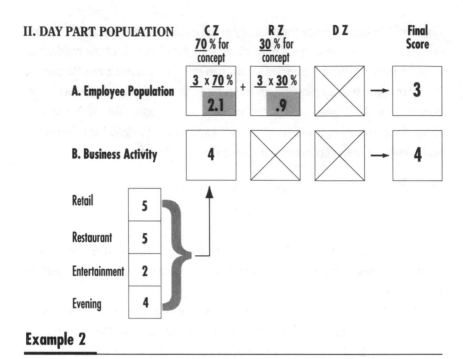

	C Z **70** % for concept	**R Z** **30** % for concept	**D Z**	**Final** **Score**
A. Employee Population	$\dfrac{3 \times 70\%}{2.1}$ +	$\dfrac{3 \times 30\%}{.9}$	☒ →	**3**
B. Business Activity	**4**	☒	☒ →	**4**

Retail	5
Restaurant	5
Entertainment	2
Evening	4

Example 2

Sample worksheet for employee population and business activity.

In order to best evaluate business activity, it helps to first assess the individual factors that will contribute to your rating. This information is available on some demographic reports or can be based on your own observations.

Retail Activity: Rate the retail activity in the area around the site.
- 5 Major activity center
- 4 Good activity center
- 3 Moderate activity center
- 2 Limited activity center
- 1 Poor activity center

Restaurant Activity: Rate the restaurant activity in the area around the site.
- 5 This is where everyone goes to eat out (a restaurant row)
- 4 One of the best areas to go when dining out
- 3 A good or logical area to go when dining out

2 A fair area to go when dining out

1 A poor area for dining out

Entertainment Activity: Rate the entertainment activity in the area around the site.

5 Premier (One of the best areas for entertainment in the market)

4 Excellent

3 Good

2 Fair

1 Poor

Evening Activity: Rate the amount of evening (after 7 p.m.) retail, dining, or entertainment activity in the area around the site.

5 Premier

4 Extremely active

3 Good activity

2 Fair activity

1 Little or no activity

Now you are ready to enter a final business activity rating for the convenience zone. You should base this evaluation on the ratings entered for each of the four individual activity categories (retail, restaurant, entertainment, and evening activity); however, as was the case with resident fit, it may be best to avoid simply averaging the scores in the individual categories. Use your own experience and the concepts outlined in Chapter 7 to determine which of the business activity categories are most important to your concept. For example, if your concept is a coffee bar, restaurant and evening activity will likely be more important than retail activity.

With this in mind, use the following scale to rate the level of business activity in the retail trade area around your site.

5 High level of activity

4 Good level of activity

3 Moderate level of activity

2 Some activity

1 Little to no activity

This is your final business activity rating. Enter this number in the appropriate box (see Example 2, page 124).

C. Transient Population

In evaluating the impact of the transient population, you will be rating the level of impact that both commuters and travelers will have on your site. Because only commuters and transients in the immediate area around your site can be potential customers, we need to consider only the convenience zone. First, consider the individual impact of commuters and travelers.

Commuter Potential: Rate how well the retail business area in the convenience zone represents a realistic place for commuters to stop.

5 This is a major thoroughfare for commuters and travelers
4 It is a natural, convenient place to stop
3 It is a fairly convenient place to stop
2 It is only slightly convenient to stop
1 It is not convenient at all to stop

Traveler Influence: Rate the potential of this site to attract travelers (people in transit through the city). In making your judgment, consider the volume of travelers on the roads near the site and the likelihood that a traveler will actually note the signage, be able to exit, and come to this site.

5 Excellent
4 Good
3 Fair
2 Slight
1 None

Now you are ready to enter a final transient population rating for the convenience zone. Consider the impact of both commuters and travelers and then assign a final rating that reflects the relative importance of each of these categories on your site. For example, if you are a doughnut shop located on the way to work, commuters will likely impact your business more than travelers. However, if you are a gas station on the interstate, travelers will be a more important consideration for you. It may be helpful to review Chapter 8 for additional information.

With this in mind, use the following scale to rate the volume of transients available to your concept in the convenience zone.

5 Abundant
4 Good
3 Adequate
2 Fair
1 Sparse

This is your final score for the transient population. Enter this number in the appropriate box.

D. Employee Fit

Use the following scale to rate the portion of the employees in the convenience and residential zone who are likely to fit your customer profile.

5 All
4 Most
3 Some
2 A few
1 None

Multiply both ratings by the respective number entered as "___ % for concept" in the calculation for Employee Population (see II-A). The resulting number is the final employee fit rating for that zone. Enter this number in the shaded box in the lower right corner of each cell. The final score for employee fit is determined by adding together the final ratings for both zones. The resulting employee fit score should be between 1 and 5. Enter this number in the appropriate box.

E. Shopper Fit

Use the following scale to rate the portion of shoppers in the convenience zone who are likely to fit your customer profile.

> 5 All
> 4 Most
> 3 Some
> 2 A few
> 1 None

This is your final score for shopper fit. Enter this number in the appropriate box.

F. Transient Fit

Use the following scale to rate the portion of transients traveling through the convenience zone who are likely to fit your customer profile.

> 5 All
> 4 Most
> 3 Some
> 2 A few
> 1 None

This is your final score for transient fit. Enter this number in the appropriate box.

III. COMPETITION

A. Demand

Before the impact of competition can be assessed, you must first evaluate the level of demand for your concept. Demand is created by customer sources. The higher the number of customer sources, the larger your demand is likely to be.

The first step in assessing demand for this model is to add together all final scores in Sections I and II of the model. You should be adding a total of nine different boxes. Enter this number in the Subtotal for Demand box. Now use the following scale to determine your demand rating.

Subtotal for Demand	Demand Rating
38-45	5
30-37	4
22-29	3
15-21	2
0-15	1

III. COMPETITION

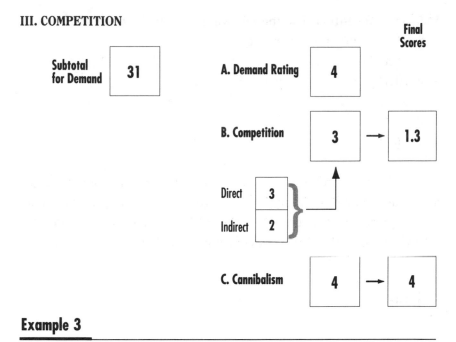

Final
Scores

Example 3

Sample worksheet for competition.

Enter this number in the Demand Rating box (see Example 3).

B. Competition

The competition rating is a measure of the direct and indirect competition for your business. First evaluate the individual impact of direct and indirect competition in the convenience zone.

Direct Competition: Use the following scale to estimate the level of direct competition for your business.

5 Excessive
4 High
3 Moderate
2 Low
1 Slight

Indirect Competition: Use the following scale to estimate the level of indirect competition for your concept.

5 Excessive
4 High
3 Moderate
2 Low
1 Slight

Use your evaluation of both direct and indirect competition to assign a general competition rating based on the scale below. Again, use your own judgment and the concepts outlined in Chapter 12 to determine the relative importance of both types of competitors to your concept.

5 Saturated
4 High
3 Moderate
2 Low
1 Slight

Enter this number in the Competition Rating box. Now calculate your final Competition Score by dividing the Demand Rating (1-5) by the Competition Rating (1-5). Enter this number in the appropriate box (see Example 3). Note that it is possible to get a final Competition Score lower than 1.

C. Cannibalism
Use the following scale to estimate the impact of cannibalism on this site.

Sales Lost to Cannibalism	Cannibalism Rating
0-5%	5
5-10%	4
10-15%	3
15-20%	2
20% or more	1

This is your final cannibalism score. Enter this number in the appropriate box.

IV. SITE FEATURES

The site features rating includes scores for both drop-in features and trade area features.

A. Drop-In Features

In evaluating drop-in features, you will be rating the convenience and potential of the site for attracting customers who make unplanned visits. Before assigning an overall drop-in rating for your site, you should first assess the five drop-in features that will contribute to your final score.

Visibility: Based on your experience in observing or evaluating the quality of other sites, how would you rate the visibility of this site from the primary road? Consider both the sign and building in making your judgment.

5 Excellent or prominent visibility
4 Good visibility
3 Fair or moderate visibility
2 Poor visibility
1 No visibility

Prototype: The building, signage, and facade of a concept communicate a distinctive image that is easy to recognize when similar to a common prototype and difficult to recognize when forced into an unusual space or building. Use the following scale to evaluate how much the image of this site will look like your typical prototype or a typical prototype for this type of business.

5 Identical to a typical prototype
4 Very similar to a typical prototype
3 A good bit like a typical prototype
2 A little different from a typical prototype
1 Quite different from a typical prototype

Access: How easy is it to get from the major traffic arteries to a convenient place to park for the site?

5 Very easy

4 Easy

3 Fairly easy

2 Somewhat difficult

1 Difficult

Strategic Position: How is the site situated relative to other businesses in the immediate area?

5 Premier or unique strategic position

4 Very good strategic position

3 Good strategic position

2 Fair strategic position

1 Weak strategic position

Parking: Rate the portion of time that convenient parking will be available.

5 All of the time

4 Most of the time (except at peak periods, around holidays, or on some weekends.)

3 A good deal of the time

2 Sometimes

1 Seldom

Now you are ready to enter a final drop-in features rating. You should base this evaluation on the ratings entered for each of the five individual drop-in features (visibility, prototype, access, strategic position, and parking). Use your own experience and the concepts outlined in Chapter 9 to determine which of the drop-in features are most important to your concept and weight these accordingly. For example, if you are a convenience concept, visibility and access may be most important, while if you are a destination concept, strategic position may be more important.

Based on this information, assign an overall rating for this site's drop-in features.

5 Excellent drop-in features

4 Very good drop-in features

3 Good drop-in features

2 Fair drop-in features

1 Poor drop-in features

This is your final score for drop-in features. Enter this number in the appropriate box.

B. Trade Area Features

In evaluating trade area features, you will be rating the potential of the surrounding area around the site, access patterns from major customer sources, and some general market features. Before assigning an overall trade area features rating for your site, you should first assess the five individual trade area categories that will contribute to your final score.

Quality of Surroundings: Rate the quality of the surrounding area. Consider activity, age, safety, and other features that add to the perceived quality of the surrounding area.

5 Premier

4 Excellent

3 Good

2 Fair

1 Poor

Growth: Indicate the level of growth in this area.

5 This is a high growth area

4 This area is actively growing

3 This area continues to grow slowly

2 This area is built out, but not growing

1 This area is in decline

Resident Access: Rate the quality of the access corridor between the major residential areas and the site.

5 Excellent
4 Very good
3 Good
2 Fair
1 Poor

Employee Access: Rate the quality of the access corridor between the offices, factories, or other employment sources and the site.

5 Excellent
4 Very good
3 Good
2 Fair
1 Poor

Business Cluster: How much like your concept's customers are the people who are likely to shop at the other stores and restaurants in the immediate retail trade area.

5 Very much
4 Quite a lot
3 Somewhat similar
2 A little similar
1 Not very similar

Now you are ready to enter a final trade area features rating. You should base this evaluation on the ratings entered for each of the five individual trade area features. Use your own experience and the concepts outlined in Chapters 10 and 11 to determine which of the trade area categories are most important to your concept and weight these accordingly. For example, if you are a convenience concept, the quality of the surrounding business cluster or resident access may be most important, while if you are a destination concept, the physical environment may be more important.

Based on this information, use the following scale to assign an overall rating for trade area features.

5 Excellent trade area features
4 Very good trade area features
3 Good trade area features
2 Fair trade area features
1 Poor trade area features

This is your final score for trade area features. Enter this number in the appropriate box.

STEP F: APPLYING APPROPRIATE WEIGHTS

The final scores you have entered in the model are a fairly sound evaluation of the factors influencing the quality of a site because they represent a number of relevant objective and subjective factors in your judgments. They are not the most accurate evaluation, however, because they are not *weighted* on the basis of their relative importance. A **weight** is simply a measure of the relative value of a particular feature. As discussed in earlier chapters, certain factors and features are more important to some concepts than to others. For example, it is not surprising that the weight or relative importance of drop-in features is greater for convenience concepts than for destination concepts.

The final evaluation of site quality depends on assigning weights to each demographic and site feature and producing an overall site quality score. The following tables provide a starting set of relative weights for convenience and destination concepts. Simply multiply your final score in each category by the appropriate relative weight to get a final weighted score. Your raw site quality score is calculated by adding up all of the weighted scores. Step G (page 138) then provides the necessary information for converting your raw score into a final site quality estimate.

Although there are many years of research behind the assigned relative weights, they are not the final word. Rather, they are designed to be used as a starting point for assigning your own relative weights. As the best expert on your customers and your business, you should have the final say as to which features are most critical to the success of your site.

Suggested Relative Weights for Convenience Concepts

Category	Final Score		Suggested Relative Weight		Final Weighted Score
Neighborhood Population	_____	(X)	10	=	_____
Special Population	_____	(X)	2	=	_____
Resident Fit	_____	(X)	12	=	_____
Employee Population	_____	(X)	5	=	_____
Business Activity	_____	(X)	7	=	_____
Transient Population	_____	(X)	10	=	_____
Employee Fit	_____	(X)	5	=	_____
Shopper Fit	_____	(X)	5	=	_____
Transient Fit	_____	(X)	5	=	_____
Competition	_____	(X)	16	=	_____
Cannibalism	_____	(X)	3	=	_____
Drop-in Features	_____	(X)	20	=	_____
Trade Area Features	_____	(X)	8	=	_____

Raw Site Quality Score   _____

Suggested Relative Weights for Destination Concepts

Category	Final Score		Suggested Relative Weight		Final Weighted Score
Neighborhood Population	_____	(X)	8	=	_____
Special Population	_____	(X)	2	=	_____
Resident Fit	_____	(X)	17	=	_____
Employee Population	_____	(X)	6	=	_____
Business Activity	_____	(X)	9	=	_____
Transient Population	_____	(X)	5	=	_____
Employee Fit	_____	(X)	8	=	_____
Shopper Fit	_____	(X)	4	=	_____
Transient Fit	_____	(X)	2	=	_____
Competition	_____	(X)	20	=	_____
Cannibalism	_____	(X)	5	=	_____
Drop-in Features	_____	(X)	14	=	_____
Trade Area Features	_____	(X)	10	=	_____

Raw Site Quality Score   _____

STEP G: EVALUATING YOUR SITE: TRADE OFFS AND NEGOTIATIONS

Your final site quality score is calculated by dividing your raw site quality score by five and then using the following scale to determine a site quality estimate.

Raw Site Quality Score ÷ 5 = Final Site Quality Score

Site Quality Score	Site Quality Estimate
89 or above	Excellent
77-88	Above Average
64-76	Average
51-63	Fair
22-50	Dog

The reality of doing a site evaluation is that the *process* means at least as much as the *score*. As emphasized throughout the book, the interactions between your strategy, site and neighborhood features, and the special circumstances associated with any site decision may be much more important than the sum of the weights. The exceptions _are_ the rule. You may decide to ditch an "A" site because it's too expensive to produce a return on your investment or because you may soon be outpositioned. On the other hand, you may decide to take a site with only an average score because you feel certain that high growth will soon make this a strategic location. For example, consider how the simple awareness of the following dynamics might affect your interpretation of a final site evaluation score.

- Convenience-oriented concepts need a high rating on the specific site feature score to succeed, regardless of the other features.

- Strategic position is crucial in highly competitive markets.

- Neighborhood-oriented destination concepts can trade visibility and access for good position relative to the customer base. On the other hand, concepts that depend on commuters or transients must have good visibility and access.

- In a new market, your marketing strategy may be much more important than the location you select.

- High market penetration increases the importance of specific site features as each location becomes more driven by convenience factors.

All of these factors are too complex and variable to include directly in any model. Unfortunately, they also mean that despite our best efforts to create an objective evaluation tool, we are still faced with subjective issues in the final site decision.

The important point is that you consider all possible positive and negative interactions before making a final decision. One of the most effective ways to identify important negative interactions (*or red flags*) is to ask the right questions. Here are some examples that have proven their value.

Red Flags

1. Does the site meet the requirements of my strategic plan or at least the principles established to guide site selection? This is a crucial question. If not, what objective or subjective reasons justify an exception?

2. Is this an atypical site compared to other locations?

3. Are the demographics unusual or atypical compared to other locations?

4. Does it have unusual features or problems (such as construction or a high crime rate) that you must assume will not be an issue once the store is opened?

5. Is the quality of this site contingent on something else happening (such as finishing construction on the mall across the street)?

6. Is the amount of competition unusually high or unusually low?

7. Are nearby neighborhoods in decline (vacant, boarded-up homes, etc.)?

8. Is this a new market?

9. Did the retail trade zone decline over the past five years?

10. Did another business fail in this location?

11. Why didn't a competitor take this location earlier?

12. Are the drop-in features fair or poor?

13. Is this site adjacent to vacant land or office buildings?

14. Are the other businesses around my site active during the period I expect to be open?

15. Does this location have a geographic barrier (e.g., a river or interstate that's difficult to get across) or a perceived ethnic or cultural boundary that shrinks the actual trade area?

Red flags are an early warning system for possible problems. You are free to ignore them (and you will want to do just that in many situations), but you will sleep much better if you do so intentionally, with a clear reason for your choice.

While it is crucial to consider all possible red flags before making a final decision, you will also want to give consideration to green lights, or those interactions that will increase the likelihood of a business doing well at a particular location.

GREEN LIGHTS

1. A major, direct competitor is doing well near your proposed site.

2. You are considering a densely populated market with limited competition and a history of good support for your type of concept.

3. The site is in a strong strategic position in an affluent, growing part of the market.

4. Your market presence is so strong that any location in the market tends to be successful.

5. This area shows excellent balance between residents, employees, and shoppers (all of whom fit your customer profile), and the site's drop-in features are strong enough to attract them.

6. The area itself is a tremendous draw because of business or entertainment factors.

7. There's a high level of demand in the area, but there isn't another place to get your product for 100 miles.

Of course, the total possible set of circumstances and issues is unlimited. The following chapter presents some important points to keep in mind when you are dealing with specific circumstances, such as opening your first convenience concept in a new market, or adding a second store.

Chapter 15

Practical Advice from the Field

Each concept, each market, each situation is different. When you are the only game in town, drop-in features may not matter. When you are a convenience concept located next to Disney World, who cares if there is no support from the local neighborhood? When you are adjacent to the best neighborhood in the city, but separated by a barrier like the Great Wall of China, look out. And finally, when your six-year-old demographic report tells you no one but farmers lives in the trade area, yet you are standing in the middle of the highest growth area of town surrounded by a sea of new homes—you ignore the report.

As you make real decisions about real sites, special considerations are the rule, not the exception. In any situation, you must account for the interaction between your type of concept, your development plans, the neighborhood, office and retail activity, trade area growth, site features, and drop-in features. In the following sections, I present a few important points to keep in mind when you are dealing with some specific circumstances, such as opening your first convenience concept in a new market, or adding a second store. Of course, the total possible set of circumstances and issues is unlimited. I am listing only a few.

KEY POINTS FOR CONVENIENCE BUSINESSES IN GENERAL

1. Neighborhood and employee demographics don't matter as much. Sales are usually driven by a broad range of demographic groups.

2. Visibility, access, and parking are very important!

3. Good position in the trade area is the key. A weaker position can work if demand is very high and drop-in features are good.

4. Being on the going-home or going-to-work side of the road may be crucial if you depend on commuter business.

5. Customer sources do not need to be balanced if one source (such as transients or local employees) is very strong.

6. Infrequent users may drive sales in transient locations, but frequent or regular usage is the key. Linkages with other errands or activities help with frequency.

KEY POINTS FOR DESTINATION BUSINESSES IN GENERAL

1. Neighborhood and employee demographics are very important. Sales are usually driven by several specific demographic groups.

2. Infrequent users are the key to high sales. Frequent users are important, but a strong base of infrequent customers guarantees success in the face of increased competition within the local retail area.

3. Visibility is important, especially for infrequent users. Access and parking are less important. Parking may have a ceiling effect on sales, but unless it is generally poor, it won't lead to low sales.

4. Good position in the trade area is important, but not essential as long as it is offset by strong marketing to build local awareness and good drop-in features; however, high competition will erode sales over time even when other factors are good.

5. Being on the going-home or going-to-work side of the road is largely irrelevant, even if you depend on commuter business. As a destination, if customers can see you, they will usually take the trouble to get to your store.

6. The best locations will have balanced customer sources (residents, employees, trade area draw). You may have a successful site if one source is very strong, but your risk also increases.

THE FIRST LOCATION IN THE MARKET FOR A DESTINATION CONCEPT

1. Think strategically. Avoid locating in the middle of two potential trade areas that will each need a store when you expand in the market.

2. Signage and a prominent position on a heavily traveled road are a terrific way to build awareness before you can use media cost-effectively

in the market. Be willing to spend the money for this type of exposure.

3. Act like a destination. Don't wait for customers to find you. Give every potential customer in the market an excuse to visit you in the first six months. It is much more important to build early connections with these infrequent users than to market heavily to frequent users. This latter group will find you regardless.

4. Visibility is more important than access; strategic position is more important than visibility.

5. Look for a good balance between residential, employee, and retail customer sources. Risk increases if one of these is weak. Transients are a plus in this location but should not drive your decision.

ADDING THE SECOND STORE IN A MARKET

1. If your first store is local and has limited awareness in the market, go from your existing trade area to a contiguous area. Don't be too concerned about some cannibalism.

2. If your first store is a destination, contiguity is not an issue. Add the second store in the trade area that is best from a strategic perspective.

3. Look for locations with moderate competition and strong draws. You want exposure to more of the market, quickly. Later you will seek out the riskier locations with low competition and uncertain draw.

4. Give careful attention to neighborhood demographics in all but the strongest retail and office areas. Over time, your fit with the neighborhood residents will have a strong impact on sales.

BACKFILLING IN A SATURATED MARKET

1. Now you are looking for pockets of customers not adequately served by your other locations. Neighborhood demographics are the key; areas with strong business and retail activity will probably have already been selected.

2. You are looking for neighborhoods with an adequate population of your customers. Demographics based on customer segments can be invaluable here for targeting specific households.

3. Research on the origins and destinations of customers in existing stores can be a big help in defining trade areas and evaluating cannibalism.

4. Competition is probably not a major concern. If you are backfilling, you are already a major player and planning to overwhelm the competition through a convenience strategy (see the next item).

5. As your locations become more and more prevalent throughout the market, even destination concepts become convenience oriented by default. Sales in all stores will begin to depend more and more on drop-in features, especially proximity to a freeway or other major access corridors in the market.

ENTERING A MARKET WITH NO COMPETITION

1. In contiguous markets (if you already have stores open), you will have established adequate levels of awareness. In new or distant markets, an investment in some market research can prevent a disaster.

2. Always ask, "Why is there no competition?" and be comfortable with the answer before you proceed.

3. The better the market for your concept, the sooner you will have strong competition. Select a good strategic position now and avoid being outpositioned later.

4. Take a deep breath and exhale slowly—the key issues underlying success in new markets are often not related to site selection, but rather to regional perceptions of your concept and marketing. Be sure your company has its marketing and operational strategy in order so that the responsibility for sales is properly shared.

ENTERING A MARKET WITH HEAVY COMPETITION

1. Saturated markets require some special planning. To be successful in such a market you must displace other competitors or be satisfied with below average sales. You can also assume that eventually (perhaps soon) there will be a "shake-out."

2. If you want a few locations to build market presence, pay what it takes to acquire strong strategic positions in competitive areas still achieving good sales. These types of locations are less affected by the competition.

3. A second strategy is to acquire strategic locations in new areas of the market and wait for the shake-out to find locations in competitive areas.

4. Do not enter a highly competitive market without a strong, coordinated marketing and development strategy—that is, unless you have deep pockets and enjoy being punched in the stomach repeatedly.

5. Be patient. Good locations or even average locations are difficult to find. The longer you wait, the better your chance of buying out a competitor with good locations or avoiding the shakeout.

6. Population density is a key variable in your site evaluations. Areas with high population density are much more forgiving about less desirable locations. City folks are used to the pain of inconvenience for destination concepts because real estate is so hard to obtain.

Chapter 16

A Final Word

So now you've done it. You ordered the demographics you needed; you decided on your plans and priorities; you drove the neighborhood and collected the necessary field data; and you completed the site evaluation model and generated a final score. And—

Your site scored a 57 on the 1-110 scale of site quality!

"That's great," you think. "My site—the one that I worked weeks to locate and research; the one I negotiated with the owner, the other tenants, seven city officials, and the mayor's brother; the one that I've convinced my company to purchase or lease—scored only 57!? There must be a mistake. Let me check that score again. Perhaps the neighborhood demographics are really excellent and I only gave them a good rating. Visibility must be at least average even though you can't see the building from the street. This is a great site. The model must be biased."

I opened the book describing a site in Oklahoma and the different perspectives on that site that each interested party had. In finishing the book, I come back to the same place. All of the information on principles, context and site features, all of the field work and demographic reports, and all of the site questions, ratings, and scores still feed into what is ultimately a very human, very subjective, and very personal process. A yes or no decision about the site must be made, and a fundamental conflict of interest is likely because, in most cases, *the person evaluating the site will benefit most if the site receives a good evaluation*. This is true in all of the following cases.

1. You are the broker who selected this site for a client.

2. You are part of a (or "the") real estate team for a corporation and your reputation in the company depends in part on how many sites you locate each year.

3. You are an owner who wants to use the site report for leverage with potential investors.

4. You are an executive responsible to your stockholders for a certain level of annual growth.

5. You own the site and want to sell it.

6. You are a business owner looking for a good location, and you think you have found it.

In each of these situations you will be somewhat biased toward obtaining a good evaluation. In each case you will be disappointed with a site evaluation score that is average or worse. After all, you wouldn't have selected the site if you hadn't expected at least a good rating.

Several years ago, Tangram built a model for a retail client. When the model was delivered and tested on some potential locations in Chicago, the director of real estate called and said, "I ran the model on several sites. The scores are too low. I need you to 'fix' the model." Further conversation revealed that the real estate staff had already made commitments to purchase the two sites and now needed to "sell" the sites to the corporation's executive committee. They were concerned because the site model did not corroborate a decision that was already made. Despite the model's low predictions, the sites were purchased and the new stores opened. Three years later the sales still have not reached expectations.

This doesn't mean that following the process in the book guarantees that your site evaluation scores will always be "right," but it does illustrate a common problem around the use of any type of objective information. We may only want it when it supports our present view.

As we move from the corporate team with many sites to evaluate to the broker or business owner with one site to evaluate, the consequences of a single mistake in site selection become much greater. Yet, in my experience, the tendency to ignore or resist negative information is not diminished. The reasons for this have to do both with the level of personal involvement and the need to sell others (banks, investors, owners) on the value of this property. Unfortunately, when an objective site evaluation is used in this biased manner—considered when it supports prevailing opinion and ignored when it disagrees—its power as a decision-making tool is greatly diminished and its role in the real estate process becomes adversarial. If the site evaluation conflicts with expectations, the evaluation process (or model) is suspect. If it supports expectations, then the process is redundant and unnecessary.

Ultimate acceptance of an objective site evaluation often requires a shift in how the evaluation process or model is perceived. For example, I believe that an independent opinion—negative or positive—is always valuable. The model for objective site evaluation described in this book and the creation of a "score" for a particular site is nothing more than a type of highly refined information to be used and balanced with all other sources of information. This information is an asset not an adversary. The separate scales (such as the scale for drop-in features) attempt to measure "reality" for this site. You define this reality as you collect and compile the data. If there are reasons why the data don't represent the true reality, make note of them and move on.

Once your biases are removed, the site evaluation process simply creates a standard based on experience with other successful and unsuccessful sites, to compare with the present site. A low score doesn't necessarily mean a "bad" site; it means a site that rates low on the traditional criteria used to evaluate sites. Many successful locations have below average site quality ratings, especially when unique circumstances make the traditional criteria irrelevant or less important.

A site evaluation model like the one presented in this book represents another point of view, which adds integrity and objectivity to the overall site evaluation process. In order to make the overall process as honest and objective as possible, all scores—especially low ones—need to be heard. Then, if appropriate, the logical reasons behind the model's low scores can be overruled by another logic.

As you finish this book, imagine that it is you standing on that controversial piece of dirt in the hot Oklahoma sun. You understand all of the conflicting points of view and pressures operating in this situation, but you remain committed to a single purpose: To make the most accurate, beneficial decision for the company planning to build in this location. You actually welcome the conflict that results from a low or below average site quality rating because you understand that the process of coming to terms with that report will ultimately get you closer to the truth and to the best decision. This is the reason you are so successful.

GLOSSARY

access
the ease or difficulty of ingress (coming into the store or its parking area) and egress (leaving the store and its parking area) from the major traffic arteries

business cluster
the cluster of businesses immediately surrounding your site

cannibalism
in a chain corporation, the impact (as measured by the loss of sales) that a new location will have on an existing store

commuters
individuals who do not live or work in the trade area but travel past your location each day on their way to and from work

competition
any other business a customer thinks of when making a decision to buy a product that you offer

convenience business
concepts that depend primarily on a nearby customer base that "drops-in," often for an unplanned visit. Quick-serve restaurants (QSRs), convenience stores, and service stations are some of the most common examples of convenience-oriented businesses.

convenience zone
the area (usually a one to two mile ring) in which it is very easy and practical to shop or dine at your concept because of its proximity

customer fit
how well the people living in a zone fit your customer profile

customer segment
a specific demographic group defined by features such as age, income, household size, occupation, or education

customer source
the prior location of a customer and the distance traveled by that customer to come to a restaurant or retail location

day parts
the time of day in which the customer dines or shops

daytime population
people who shop or work in the vicinity of your store

demand
the actual volume of customers available for your concept

destination zone
the area outside of the trade area that provides additional customers for your concept

destination business
concepts that attract their customers, in part, through their uniqueness. Visits to a destination business are often planned ahead of time and may involve driving ten or more miles, depending on the attractiveness and availability of the concept.

direct competition
businesses that are very much like your concept in that their theme, merchandise, food, or target customer is similar to yours

drop-in access
convenience-driven access

drop-in features
specific features, such as visibility, prototype, access, parking, and strategic position that attract customers who make unplanned visits

edge location
a location near the boundary of a strip center, mall pad, or retail trade zone, with vacant land, low-income housing, or other nonsupportive development on the other side of the boundary

employee access
measures the convenience of the immediate trade area to individuals coming from work

employees
people employed in the trade area who connect a visit to your store with work

enjoyment seekers
people in the area for movies, theme parks, lakes or other natural attractions, or any other form of entertainment

great evening fallacy
a concept that depends on evening business opens a location in an area that has no evening business, assuming that they will be the draw to attract evening activity

image
a broad concept that describes all of the features that influence a customer's perception of your business, including drop-in features, physical surroundings, and market presence

indirect competition
competition that comes from stores that sell your concept as a small part of their overall business or stores that sell goods similar to yours, but with a different theme, price, quality level, or selection

ingress
coming into the store or its parking area from the major traffic arteries

law of compensation
the false assumption that low business volume in one day part will be "compensated" with strong business in another day part

linkages
businesses that relate in a way that supports the multiple needs of the consumer

market
a metropolitan statistical area (MSA), or if the area's population is too small to be classified as an MSA, the town and its surrounding residential neighborhoods

market penetration
the degree to which your present store locations "penetrate" or exhaust the potential supply of customers

market fit
the appropriateness of the market for a particular concept

model
a simplified description of some part of reality that is conveniently placed in a computer or on a worksheet so that it is accessible for use

new car fallacy
the tendency of company staff or owners to overrate their concept's visibility

primary road
the street that the building facade is designed to face

prototype
the standard building or signage configuration for your concept

regional awareness
how well you are known outside of your primary market

resident access
measures the convenience for residents in the neighborhoods around the
site to travel to the site's immediate trade area

residential zone
the demographic zone beginning at the outside edge of the convenience
zone and continuing to the outside edge of your trade area

residents
people living in the trade area

retail trade zone
the retail activity area a customer would visit to find your business. The
retail trade zone can be as small as an individual strip center or as large
as several square miles when the area includes several malls and a large
collection of shops and restaurants

sales forecasting
the process of predicting sales volume for a particular location

secondary road
the nearest cross street from which the site, building, or signage
is visible

shopper/entertainment access
measures the convenience of the site to nearby malls, entertainment centers, or concentrations of shoppers, diners, or fun seekers within one mile

shoppers
people who are shopping in the area and then come to your store, or leave
your store and continue to shop in the area

site evaluation
the objective assessment of the quality or suitability of a piece of real
estate for a specific retail or restaurant concept

site quality
the quality of a piece of real estate, taking into account demographics, site features (such as visibility and access), and competition

special populations
customer sources generated by unique circumstances, such as a university, military base, resort, or seasonal resident population

strategic access
measures the convenience of the store's position in the market relative to key customer sources

strategic position
how well (or poorly) your site is situated in the immediate retail area relative to other businesses

tourists
travelers who stop and spend time in the area

trade area
the area containing 70 to 80 percent of your customers

traffic
the volume of traffic on the primary roads, secondary roads, and freeways near the site

transient access
measures the convenience of the site to the major highways used by travelers

transients
customers who neither live in the area, work in the area, nor shop or run errands in the area, but are passing through and elect to stop

travelers
individuals in transit through the area who stop because they see your sign and your business fits the needs of a traveler

virtual zone
a nonmeasurable zone that describes the origins of customers in transit through the trade area

visibility
the degree to which your store is discriminable from surrounding stores

weight
a measure of the relative value of a particular feature

INDEX

access, 7, 38-39, 41, 44, 53, 58, 59,
  60, 64, 68-69, 72, 77, 89,
  102, 103, 104, 105, 117,
  132, 138, 139, 143, 144,
  145, 155
access and
  drop-in features, 69-70, 156
  employees, 70, 117, 134, 156
  residents, 70, 117, 133-134, 158
  shoppers, 70, 158
  strategic position, 70-71, 159
  transients, 71, 159
age, 41, 45, 46, 115, 119, 120-121
apartments, 38, 39, 41, 107
backfilling, 146
balance, 39, 77, 141, 96-99, 143,
  144, 145
basic principles, 18-21
block groups, 39
business activity, 104, 107, 110, 116,
  123-124, 136, 137, 140, 142, 146
business cluster, 37, 42, 78, 89, 96,
  108, 117, 134, 155
buying power, 41, 45, 115, 119, 121
cannibalism, 28, 94-95, 129, 130-131,
  136, 137, 145, 146, 155
category killer, 25, 27
census data, 36, 37, 44, 45
census tracts, 45, 48
chain concepts, 82, 88, 94
commuters, 24, 49, 58-59, 72, 107,
  138, 143, 144, 155
competition, 7, 23, 28, 31-33, 41,
  44, 45, 53, 59, 70, 72, 81, 83,
  87-100, 106, 108-109, 111, 128-
  131, 136, 137, 140, 145, 146,
  147, 155
competition and
  balance, 96-99
  benefits of, 88, 90, 96, 97, 98, 108
  dynamics of, 88-91
  market presence, 99
  strategic position, 99

competition, direct, 32, 89, 92,
  93-94, 96, 98, 99, 108, 111,
  129, 140, 156
competition, high, 6, 72, 88, 90, 99,
  138, 144, 147-148
competition, indirect, 32, 92-94,
  129, 130, 157
competition, low, 7, 88, 89, 96, 100,
  141, 145, 146-147
competition report, 37
convenience concepts, 12-13, 25, 27,
  32, 138
convenience concepts and
  access, 5, 69, 70, 143
  balance, 39
  customer sources, 27, 36,
    39, 110, 143
  defining, 12-13
  demographic zones 37-39, 43,
    49-50, 114
  drop-in features, 12, 64, 138,
    143, 146
  gridlock, 77
  image, 90, 91
  key recommendations for, 143
  linkages, 25-26, 143
  market for, 17
  market penetration, 83
  model for, 114,
  parking, 143
  percentage for concept, 118
  position, 39, 41, 143
  relative weights, 136
  sample worksheet, 119
  trade area, 17, 143
  traffic, 5
  visibility, 5, 44, 143
convenience zone, 36, 37-39, 40,
  41, 49, 53, 114, 155
clusters (see business clusters)
crime, 75, 76, 78, 109, 110, 139
customer behavior, 19, 22-30, 105,
  146

customer fit, 40, 42, 76, 112, 145, 155
customer knowledge, 22-30, 105
customer perspective, 110
customer segments, 41-42, 84, 112, 146, 155
customer sources, 23-25, 31, 32, 36-51, 52-57, 58-61, 71, 73, 95, 106-107, 143-148, 155
day parts, 26-28, 155
day part population, 122-128
daytime population, 27, 45, 52-57, 156
daytime population report, 45
demand, 28, 31-33, 45, 77, 88, 89, 90, 97, 98, 99, 100, 104, 111, 128-129, 141, 156
demand/shopping report, 45
demographic reports, 22, 41, 45-51, 54, 74, 111, 113, 142
demographic rings, 39, 43, 46, 48
demographics, 6, 7, 38, 44, 75, 78, 99, 105, 111-112, 139, 143, 145, 146
demographic services, 36-37, 53
demographic zones, 36-45
destination concepts, 12-13, 27, 32
destination concepts and
    access, 39, 69-70, 71, 138, 144, 145
    competition, 90, 91, 93
    customer sources, 27, 36, 53, 110, 143-144, 145
    defining, 12-13
    demographic zones, 37-49, 50, 114
    drop-in features, 12, 64, 144, 146
    gridlock, 77
    growth strategy, 81
    image, 90-91
    key recommendations for, 143-144, 144-145
    linkages, 25-26, 39
    market for, 17

    market penetration, 83
    model for, 114
    parking, 144
    percentage for concept, 118
    relative weights, 137
    strategic position, 81, 138, 144, 145
    trade area for, 17
    visibility, 138, 144, 145
destination zone, 36, 40, 42-45, 49, 50, 114, 156
direct competition
    (*see competition, direct*)
directionality, 43
dog sites, 6-7, 19, 20, 27, 64, 72-73, 77, 78, 86, 88, 92, 105
drawing power, 37, 39, 42, 43, 44, 55, 60, 74, 76, 89, 97, 98, 99, 141, 145
driving the trade area, 105-111
drop-in access (*see access, drop-in*)
drop-in customers, 39, 44, 56, 59, 64, 66
drop-in features, 7, 64-73, 110, 117, 131-133, 136, 137, 140, 141, 142, 144, 146, 156
edge locations, 77-78, 109, 156
education, 41, 45, 115, 119, 121
egress, 41, 68, 69, 73, 102
employee access
    (*see access, employee*)
employee fit, 53, 107, 112, 116, 124, 136, 137
employee population, 116, 122-123, 124, 136, 137
employees, 23, 39, 41, 50, 52-53, 70, 107, 110, 111, 112, 141, 156
enjoyment seekers
    (*see entertainment*)
entertainment activity, 38, 84, 110, 116, 124-125, 141
entertainment seekers, 24, 55-56, 70, 156
environment (*see surroundings*)

ethnicity, 109, 140
evening activity, 116, 124-125
freestanding locations, 68, 76, 89
freeways, 65, 71
frequency of usage, 22, 28-30, 38, 41, 57, 112, 143, 144, 145
frequent users, 28-30, 38, 41, 42, 112, 143, 144, 145
gaps (*see market gaps*)
geographic perspectives, 16-18
great evening fallacy, 27, 157
gridlock, 69, 74, 77, 106
growth, 89, 109, 117, 133, 138, 140, 142
growth strategy, 80-81, 85, 86, 88, 89, 94
hotels, 61, 77
household size, 41, 45, 115, 119, 121
image, 31-33, 72, 74, 75, 82, 89-90, 157
income, 41, 45, 46, 115, 119, 121
indirect competition
(*see competition, indirect*)
infrequent users, 28-30, 41, 42, 50, 112, 143, 144, 145
ingress, 41, 68, 73, 102, 157
inner ring, 49-50
InSite, 12, 25, 26, 28, 30, 39, 56, 57, 59, 60, 61, 65, 68, 72, 73, 78, 82, 90, 92, 95, 99, 100
interstate locations, 60
law of compensation, 27, 157
linkages, 23, 24, 25-26, 44, 55, 56-57, 60, 96, 98, 143, 157
low-income areas, 38, 75-76, 77, 78, 109
malls, 7, 25, 37, 54-55, 65, 72, 73, 76, 77, 96, 110
market, 7, 16-17, 18, 19, 44-45, 80-86, 88, 105, 111, 113, 140, 144-148, 157
market awareness, 41, 81, 82, 83, 87, 88, 105, 144, 146
market, backfilling, 146

market expansion, 111, 144, 145-145
market fit, 80, 83-84, 157
market gaps, 83, 95
market penetration, 80, 82-83, 139, 157
market perspective, 16
market presence, 89, 90, 94, 99, 140, 147
marketing strategy, 28-30, 111, 139, 147
markets, new, 100, 139, 140, 141, 144-145, 147
middle ring, 50
model, 4-5, 9, 13, 72, 114-117, 150-151, 157
motels, 61, 77
MSA, 16
national perspective, 16
natural amenities, 110
neighborhood, 7, 36, 44, 45, 74, 75-76, 78, 109-110, 112, 113, 138, 142, 145
neighborhood population, 115, 118-122, 136, 137, 146
new car fallacy, 66-67, 157
new markets (*see markets, new*)
outer ring, 50-51
parking, 64, 68, 117, 132, 143, 144
parks, 74, 76, 110
physical environment,
(*see surroundings*)
population, 37, 44, 148
population density, 40, 148
population growth, 37, 39
position, 39, 53, 54, 55, 56, 58, 70, 72-73, 78, 89, 92, 108-109, 143, 144
position, strategic
(*see strategic position*)
primary roads, 65, 68, 71, 158
profitability, 95, 98
prototype, 64, 67-68, 80, 84-86, 117, 131, 158

real estate system, 3, 19
red flags, 76, 78
regional awareness, 80, 81, 82, 158
relative weights (*see weights*)
resident access (*see access, resident*)
resident fit, 112, 115, 119, 120-122, 136, 137, 145
resident population, 52, 72, 115, 118-122, 146
residential zone, 36, 39-42, 49, 50, 114, 158
residents, 23, 36-51, 53, 54, 61, 70, 111, 141, 158
restaurant activity, 116, 124-125
retail activity (*see business activity*)
retail balance, 77
retail trade zone, 37, 42, 44, 50, 70, 72, 73, 77, 97, 98, 99, 107, 140, 158
risk, 44, 90-91, 97, 100, 144, 145
sales forecasting, 9-10, 158
sales volume, 9, 19, 60, 64, 95, 99
schools, 29, 110
seasonal residents, 61
secondary roads, 65, 68, 71, 158
shopper fit, 54, 127-128, 136, 137
shoppers, 24, 25, 36, 38, 41, 45, 50, 54, 70, 107, 141, 158
short-term sales, 20-21,
shrinkage, 9
signage, 41, 44, 65, 66, 67, 82, 84, 85, 102-103, 144
site evaluation and
    basic principles of, 18-21, 149-152
    components of, 10-11
    context of, 3, 14-15, 149-152
    definitions of, 8-9, 158
    four perspectives of, 3, 6, 15-18
    green lights, 140-141
    language of, 3, 4, 6
    logic in, 4, 6, 8, 152
    model for, 4-5, 9-10, 72, 114-117
    objectives of, 10, 18, 150-152

objectivity in, 3, 6, 19, 32, 69, 102-103, 151-152
practical advice, 142-148
process of, 3, 4, 5, 8, 10, 20-21, 82, 102-141
red flags, 76, 78, 139-140
relativity of, 11-12
sales forecasting, 9-10
site perspective, 18
subjectivity in, 12, 69, 75, 98, 102-104, 150
trade area perspective, 16-17
worksheet for, 115-117
site features, 6, 7, 16, 64-78, 89, 104, 105, 113, 117, 131-135, 138, 139, 142
site perspective, 18
site quality, 4, 5, 6, 9, 11-12, 19, 20, 81, 105, 135, 149-152, 159
site quality estimate, 135, 138-141, 149-152
site quality score, 135, 138-141, 149, 150
special populations, 24, 61, 115, 119, 120, 136, 137, 159
specific household report, 45
strategic access
    (*see access, strategic*)
strategic plan, 14, 20-21, 86, 104-105, 113, 138, 139, 144, 145, 146, 147
strategic position, 7, 44, 60, 64, 72-73, 77, 78, 81, 92, 99, 108, 117, 132, 138, 140, 143, 145, 147, 159
strip centers, 25-26, 37, 56, 68, 73, 77, 89, 110
subjectivity, 102-104, 150
surroundings, physical, 44, 74-78, 89, 117, 133
take-out customers, 24
Tangram Corporation, 5, 15, 26, 66, 68, 114, 150

three-ring report, 46, 47, 48-51, 105
tourists, 61, 159
trade area, 16, 17, 29, 36, 39, 40, 42,
   51, 53, 55, 70, 89, 92, 98, 99,
   100, 104, 105-111, 140, 142, 144,
   145, 146, 159
trade area features, 117, 133-135,
   136, 137
trade area gaps, 83, 95
trade area perspective, 16-17
traditional report, 45
traffic, 7, 41, 44, 65, 71-72, 73, 77,
   78, 106, 108, 159
traffic, commuter, 59
traffic flow, 50, 75, 105
transient fit, 128, 136, 137
transient population, 116, 124, 126,
   136, 137

transients, 42, 54, 58-61, 107, 138,
   143, 159
travelers, 24, 25, 43, 44, 59-60, 72,
   107, 116, 126-127, 159
U.S. Census, 36, 37,
vacant land, 7, 74, 77, 78, 109, 140
virtual zone, 43, 159
visibility, 7, 11, 41, 44, 53, 58, 59,
   60, 64, 66-67, 70, 72, 73, 81, 89,
   102, 103, 104, 105, 117, 131,
   138, 139, 143, 144, 145, 159
weights, relative, 5, 12, 114,
   135-137, 138, 159
worksheet, entering data in, 114-135
worksheet, site evaluation, 106,
   115-117